WORDS & PHRASES

IN

ANGLING

From
adipose fin to zulu

Compiled by
KEN WALKER

With additional material by

POCKET REFERENCE BOOKS

Published by:
Pocket Reference Books Publishing Ltd.
Premier House
Hinton Road
Bournemouth
Dorset BH1 2EF

First published 1996

Typesetting:	Gary Tomlinson PrintRelate (Bournemouth, Dorset) (01202) 897659
Cover Design:	Van Renselar Bonney Design Associates West Wickham, Kent BR4 9QH
Printing and Binding:	RPM Reprographics Units 2-3 Spur Road Quarry Lane, Chichester West Sussex PO19 2PR Tel. 01243 787077 Fax. 01243 780012 Modem 01243 536482 E-Mail: rpm@argonet.co.uk

ISBN: 1 899437 58 4

A POCKET REFERENCE BOOK

Contents	**Pages**
A Selected Charity	Inside Front Cover
Title Page	1
Copyright, typesetting, cover design, printing and binding	2
Introduction	4
A Few Teasers	5
Angling Clubs	6
Words & Phrases in Angling (adipose fin to zulu)	7 to 124
Izaak Walton – The Compleat Angler	125 to 126
The Fish World – A Classification	127 to 128
History of Selected Charity	Inside Back Cover

INTRODUCTION – ANGLING

> *"Gaze upon the rolling deep*
> *(Fish is plentiful and cheap)*
> *As the sea my love is deep!"*
> *Said the Yonghy-Bonghy-Bo*

Edward Lear (1812-1888) wrote that in one of his fanciful poems – "The Courtship of the Yonghy-Bonghy-Bo".

YBB (we use acronyms these days) was courting Lady Jingly.

Lady Jingly rejected YBB's advances. Should she have known better?

Had she not heard of global warming?

About 70% of the earth's surface is covered by the seas, and our own islands are merely precious stones set in a silvery sea, to paraphrase William Shakespeare (I humbly beg his pardon).

In this remarkable compilation of fish, fishing terms, fishing parlance and fishing tackle, Ken Walker has produced a fascinating Pocket Reference Book which should be in the pocket or haversack of every schoolboy fishing for tadpoles, or every devoted angler probing for the predatory pike.

He has even included some of the mysteries of fishing cuisine, and tells us that perch 'rivals the trout in its flavour, and is best fried, grilled or barbecued.'

Whether you catch fish by hand (my word, you're quick), by fly, by hook, by net, or whether you squeeze the last bit out of a tin of pilchards, you must know that fish food will always sustain us.

There are over 1,000 entries in this book, and each one will fascinate you – whether novice or whaler.

There are three main groups of fishes – the jawless, the sharks and rays, and the bony ones – of which there are about 20,000 species.

Are there any more there down below?

FRANCIS COOKE

TEASERS

Black spot can be found on roses, but what about fish?

What would you do with a Colorado spoon?

Where do eels spawn?

Do you know the common name for pleuronectes flesus?

Where would you find the gillaroo?

How many kinds of shark are there?

Why should you avoid knotted nets?

Who invented the Arlesey bomb?

How far can the average angler cast?

What is a joey?

You'll find the answers, and many more questions will also be answered, in the pages that follow

---

"The gods do not subtract from the alloted space of men's lives the time spent in fishing." – ANON

SIGN ABOVE THE DOOR
OF THE AQUARIUM ON THE COBB
AT LYME REGIS, DORSET.

ANGLING CLUBS

There are hundreds of angling clubs in the British Isles, and anyone can form a club.

The main reasons for the existence of these clubs are social – it is quite pleasant, and sometimes re-assuring, to have some contact with others who share your obsession – and financial.

The financial side is important for several reasons; fishing waters are hard to find, and a club has more chance to acquire fishing rights on a stretch than an individual, as most owners will lease them on the understanding that maintenance is carried out, and the waters kept in good condition.

Clearly, a group can afford to do this more easily than an individual. Sea-angling clubs exist to spread the cost of boat hire and transport to the sea. Angling clubs exist as an adjunct to many organisations – public houses, workplaces, social clubs, and just as angling clubs.

Clubs will also be found in clubs – that is, as organisations affiliated to a larger organisation; in this case, members of one small club will usually have the right to fish on other affiliated clubs' grounds, and the opportunity arises for competitions between member clubs.

Furthermore, the large local organisations will belong to national groups, and national competitions are organised. Clubs also exist for the benefit of single-species enthusiasts, particularly among sea-anglers.

Most clubs involved in coarse fishing in the British Isles are affiliated to the National Federation of Anglers, Halliday House, Egginton, Derbyshire, DE65 6GU. You can telephone them on 01283 734735, and ask for the address of your nearest angling club.

Game fishermen are covered by the Salmon and Trout Association, Fishmongers' Hall, London EC4R 9EL, telephone 0171 283 5838.

Sea anglers are catered for by the National Federation of Sea Anglers at 51a Queen Street, Newton Abbott, Devon, TQ12 2QT. Telephone number is 01626 331330.

adipose fin – small fleshy dorsal protuberance just in front of the caudal fin (tail). It seems to serve no function, but is a recognition point of the salmonidae family.

aerator – a pump. When transporting or storing live-bait that need a good supply of oxygen in order to keep them alive, such as sandeels, a pump that will push air through the tank in which they are being kept is a necessity.

> **A.F.T.M.** – the Association of Fishing Tackle Manufacturers, to whose coding for fly-fishing lines we now subscribe. This code tells you where and what taper the line has, the weight and its position, and whether the line is a floating or a sinking line.

Alder – an artificial fly.

alevin – the young stage of the salmonidae family, for the six or so weeks immediately after hatching.

At this stage they feed on the yolk-sac they bring with them from the egg, and are prey to many species of fish; including minnows, the water-beetle and particularly the larvae of the dragonfly.

Those that survive this stage become fry, fish shaped, but with a disproportionately large head.

algae – member of the group of thallophytes, a family of sea-weeds.

Familiar to the angler in the form of a green scum on the surface, which affects the fishing in the degree to which it is too thick to penetrate, in which case it is also causing the water to lose oxygen, resulting in poor fishing.

> Blue-green algae gives rise to concern in some lakes, as it appears to be poisonous, or poisons the flesh of the fish taken from that lake. Its origins are obscure, and it is thought by some to be the result of industrial pollution.

Allis shad – *alosa alosa*, a marine fish that goes up-river to fresh water to spawn; the numbers of this once numerous fish have been depleted, mainly through pollution.

Shaped rather like a herring, with a dark grey back, pinky-silvery flanks and a silver underside, the allis shad has a brown 'thumb mark' behind the gill covers.

Still found in some estuaries, such as the Severn, most baits will take them, as will small spinners. Good eating, especially the roe. Grows to about 1kg (2.2lb).

See also Twaite Shad

anatto, annatto – yellow-orange dye-stuff sold in paste form by many tackle and bait dealers for dyeing maggots. Natural, made from the fruit-pulp of a tropical tree from the Americas and Caribbean.

AQUACULTURE

That's fish farming in modern terminology.

Fish are raised under controlled conditions in tanks and ponds, sometimes in offshore pens.

It has been practised for centuries in the Far East, where Japan alone produces about 100,000 tonnes of fish a year.

---

angler fish – *lophius piscatoris*. Ugly is the most accurate way of describing this, or rather these, fish.

There are several variants, living at varying depths, and they are all grotesque. They take their name from the method they use to catch their prey – small fish – which utilises an antenna with a glowing end that droops just in front of the angler's mouth. The prey is attracted by the glow, and approaches near enough for the angler to pounce.

They are edible, and fish bait will catch them, although it would seem that most angler fish are caught by accident when other fish were being sought.

Angler fish of over 30kg (66lb) have been caught, and a dead one of 68kg (150lb) was found floating in the sea off Ireland.

angling – the sport – or even art – of catching fish with a rod and line, as opposed to netting or trapping or, favourite sport of the British Army, stunning them with a small explosive charge.

aniseed – *anise*, seed of an aromatic plant, favoured in cookery and for the flavouring of cordials and alcoholic beverages, and much loved by dogs. Once fashionable as an additive to baits, but not now much used as such.

However, aniseed balls are pleasant to suck on a lonely vigil!

antenna float – a good float for windy conditions, with the main flotation body at the bottom, and a long quill or cane sticking up. The main body sits low in the water, giving stability, and the antenna, which offers very little windage, is a very sensitive bite indicator.

anti-kink device – a stabilising device, usually in the form of a small vane or weight, used in conjunction with a swivel, above any spinner or spoon, to stop the rotation of the bait from twisting the line.

antiques – like golf and some other sports, old items of fishing tackle and other memorabilia are now fetching ridiculous prices, which is annoying, as some pieces, such as reels, are still in usable condition, and are thus taken out of useful circulation by some collector who will own them just to look at!

True, some of the early examples are beautifully made, and are a delight to behold, and anything old is nowadays held in reverence by virtue of lasting so long in these throwaway days. However, even equipment made in the 1970s and 1980s is now considered collectable, especially if made in small numbers, or at the beginning of a fashion.

If you are the proud possessor of an old rod or reel and wish to cash in on it, the names that fetch money are Hardy (rods and reels), Farlow (reels), Fraser-Kilian (reels), Horton of Glasgow (reels) and Wilkes-Osprey (reels).

There are, of course, many more than these, and price depends on condition and the original quality of the kit, wooden and brass equipment being at a premium.

Bait boxes, fly boxes, vices, cabinets and wallets, lure boxes, any gadgets, and old gags and priests fetch good prices, while mounted fish in cases are always in demand.

Old nets, of course, should only be used for show, as the knotted type of net should not be used, for humanitarian reasons.

approach – bear in mind the fact that fish have very delicate sensory organs, particularly those of hearing and pressure.

Every heavy footfall must sound like thunder to a bream, and even heavy breathing like a gale to the notoriously sensitive chub. Approach the chosen spot on the bank with care, do not talk in loud voices, and leave the radio at home.

Remember too that you may only be there to pass the time of day in pleasant surroundings, and that catching fish may not be the sole object of the outing to you, but the fellow along the bank may think differently, and does not want the fish around his carefully ground-baited patch frightened into the next county!

If using a boat, especially in rivers or lakes, board and launch from a point well away from your intended target area, and pole or row gently to it. If you must use a motor, try to make it an electric one – and lower rather than drop your anchor.

> Keep away from anyone else, on the bank or in boats, and if trolling, row or motor gently, without splashing. It isn't a race!

Arlesey bomb – developed by Mr R. Walker, this is a pear-shaped weight used for legering, with a built-in swivel at the thin end, to the eye of which the line is attached.

artificial baits – any manufactured lure that does not include organic matter. Into this purlieu come spinners, spoons, flies, nymphs, pinks, jigs, devons, feathers and plugs.

artificial eels – originally of rubber tubing, nowadays made usually of plastic, these make good lures for bass, pollack and coalfish.

artificial nymphs – at certain times of the year, well stocked trout waters will be seen to 'bulge', that is, the trout come to the surface without breaking it.

At this time they are feeding on the nymph or larval stage of various insects that are rising to the surface, where they would throw off their casing and fly away.

Dry- or wet-flies will be useless during this period, and the wise trout angler will resort to his artificial nymphs. As the nymphs act in a way peculiar to themselves, they must be fished in a similar way. Any unnatural action will repel the trout.

The nymph rises from the bottom, so the artificial must sink to the bottom in order to rise. This is done nowadays by tying in some weight, so that it sinks, and then the line is drawn in so that it rises, is allowed to fall, then rises again, just like the behaviour of the real nymph.

Fine terminal tackle is needed, so that the trout cannot see the line and, apparently, size is of importance here, as the fish will not take anything out of the ordinary – you will need to match in size whatever nymph they are taking on the day. This is where the autopsy comes in.

The types of insect that the angler will be called upon to emulate include May-fly, dragon-fly, caddis fly, stone flies, crane fly and the gnat.

> ↑
> **CATCH 'EM QUICK!**
> These flies and their larvae are mostly found in quick-flowing streams, and here it is that they are best used.

autopsies – post-mortem examinations carried out on a specimen.

Many trout fishermen examine the stomach contents of the just caught fish in order to ascertain the type of food recently consumed, thus getting an idea of the type of fly to use at that particular time. This can involve gutting the fish, but some use an old-fashioned marrow spoon, thrust down the fish's gullet.

automatic reels – a type of fly reel that does not possess a winding handle, but in which pulling out the line winds a spring, which is then triggered to retrieve the line (this can be a very rapid retrieve).

Avon balsa – a type of float made of balsa wood, with rubber rings at the top and bottom.

Avon rod – a traditional rod, about 3.5 metres (11 or 12 feet) long, with a plain cane butt-piece, and a built-cane (also known as split-cane) middle and top sections.

The Avon rod takes its name from the Hampshire Avon, and was originally used for legering. It became a general-purpose rod, and is now built in hollow glass-fibre (GRP).

azurine – another name for the rudd (rutilus erythrophtalmus).

babbing or bobbing – the practice of fishing for eels by threading a number of lobworms onto a length of wool, making it into a bundle. This is then dangled (babbed or bobbed) on the bottom of the river with a short rod or stick, and the idea is that the eel takes the bait, and gets its teeth hooked into the thread, when it is lifted gently out of the water, care being taken not to shake the fish off until it is over a suitable receptacle.

This method comes from the Norfolk Broads and Essex, and is reputed to have originated with the Ancient Britons. Popular throughout East Anglia, being used in river estuaries.

backing line – many reels, particularly of the fixed-spool type, have a line capacity far greater than the average angler will ever need, especially if the angler is after fish that require lightweight line.

As 100 metres (110 yards) is as much as will ever be needed, or maybe 150-200 metres (160/220 yards) if beachcasting, to purchase the several hundred metres necessary to fill some spools is foolhardy.

Either use a filler (two semicircular pieces of cork or plastic) or simply wind on enough of a thicker line as a backing to bring the lighter line up to the height required to enable it to spill over the spool lip when casting, tying the lighter line securely to it.

Thus, there is enough line on the reel in the event of a big fighting fish taking off, and casting is not inhibited by the line dragging on the spool rim.

backlash – when casting with a centre-pin, drum-type reel, or a multiplier, if control is not kept over the speed of revolution, the reel keeps spinning when the cast is completed, and this results in a bird's nest or tangle that can take hours to sort.

This is most common when legering or boat-fishing with heavy weights, and seems to happen mostly on cold days, when fingers are least able to sort out the mess!

See page 21 for centre-pin reel, used for boat fishing or on your local pier.

back shotting – method of sinking the line above the float (when so desired) by pinching on one or two small shot about 60cm (2ft) above the float.

bailiff – the duties of a water bailiff vary from place to place. In some areas, he is responsible for the management of the fishery, in others he is just a fee-collector and unofficial policeman.

> **bait** – anything that can attract a fish to bite at it, thus impaling itself on the hook to which the bait is attached.
> Various items that are the natural food of the fish, or artefacts that simulate that food, can be used, and even substances that would appear totally unnatural, such as lengths of wool, rubber bands, luncheon meat, hempseed, feathers, aluminium foil – items that the average fish would not normally encounter in his everyday life – seem to exert a fatal fascination for some species.

bait dropper – a container, usually with holes to allow the feed-bait to escape, that is fixed to the end of the tackle, enabling a prescribed area to be baited, attracting fish to that area, in the hope that the bait on the hook will be picked up by a fish feeding on the free meal provided.

bait waiter – any tray or box-lid used to hold accessories and bait boxes conveniently to hand – available also ready-made.

baited spoon – a spoon bait with a worm or strip of fish added to the hook.

bale arm – also known as a 'pick-up', the wire loop or arm that revolves in front of a fixed-spool reel, retrieving the line and winding it around the spool.

ballan wrasse – *abrus bertgylta,* the largest and most widespread of the wrasse family in British waters. All the wrasse are beautifully marked, with the colours varying according to environment, but predominantly they are green/brown on the back and sides, merging into a reddish belly, with white spots.

The shape is similar to the carp, but stubbier, and the mouth is distinctive, with thick, muscular lips, which it uses to rip limpets and other shellfish from the rocks on which it browses.

Small fish will be found inshore, but the larger specimens take to the deeper water.

Warm-water fish, ballan wrasse can grow to 2.75-3.6kg (6-8lb), and shellfish bait fished on a sunny day on light tackle should take them. Use light tackle, wrasse should be brought to the surface gently, as they have no mechanism to equalise pressure when brought up from the deeps, so they can get the bends, and die even if released back into the sea.

They also have a reputation for 'giving up the ghost' no matter how gently they are treated. Ragworm and live prawn are favourite bait, and, oddly enough, limpet, although their everyday food of choice, does not seem to work on the hook. As to whether wrasse are edible, opinions vary, but it is generally said that they take on the flavour of whatever they have been feeding on, although it is difficult to see how those who so declare can know what the fish's diet has been, or what it tastes like!

bank stick – accessory pointed at one end to stick into the river or lake bank, threaded at the other end to accept a bait waiter, rod rest, or any other device.

barbel – *barbus barbus,* a member of the cyprinid (carp) family, the barbel is a slim, long, rounded fish, with a flattened belly, the back being grey/brown or green/brown (usually following the colour of the river-bed on which it lives), and the sides bronzed.

There are two pairs of barbels on the top lip. It prefers fast-flowing, clean rivers with a hard bottom, and gravitates towards gravelly areas. Widespread in western Europe except for Scandinavia, Denmark, Ireland, and the southern peninsulas, the barbel was, in England, found in the south-eastern counties, but has been introduced to northern rivers, and westwards to the Severn.

Feeding on molluscs, insects, worms, silkweed (larger specimens will take small fish), the barbel when young can be mistaken for the gudgeon, which is of a similar shape.

This fish, however, can reach 6.5-7.5kg (14-16lb), and is a most exciting quarry to catch, best baits being lobworm, sausage, bread and maggots, and hempseed have been taken. Legering is perhaps the favoured method, but float-fishing with fairly heavy tackle has been successful, and a good deal of ground-bait or use of a swim-feeder is recommended.

A fighting fish, the barbel needs a fairly large hook – size 14 or slightly larger, or when baiting with silkweed, up to a number 8 – a stout rod with an all-through action, and a reel that can carry up to a hundred yards of 6 to 8lb line.

Once you have caught him (or her), put him (or her) back for others to enjoy. They aren't worth eating, and the roe of the female is reputedly poisonous, especially during the spawning season, late May or early June.

basking shark – *cetorhinus maximus,* a large shark, probably the largest found in British waters, that feeds only on plankton.

It spends most of its time near the surface, hence its name, and is of absolutely no interest to the angler, as it is difficult to get a piece of plankton on a hook. Not a sporting fish.

bass – *dicentrachus labrax,* the only member of the sea-perch family (serranidae) found in British waters.

Related to the freshwater perch, this silvery, swift-moving fish is gregarious when young, when it shoals, and, in reflection of this is often known as the schoolie. It becomes more solitary when older, moving about in small numbers rather than large schools, and its colouration becomes less brilliant, taking on a darker sheen.

The schoolie will weigh up to about 1kg (2.2lb). This probably represents an age of about seven to eight years in this slow growing species, which does not become sexually mature until it is about six years old. Older fish can reach 8kg (17lb).

Predominantly found close to shore, the bass loves areas with fast currents or tide-races, and around rocky places that harbour the crabs and smaller fish that make up their diet. They are voracious predators, and may be taken on a variety of baits, particularly peeler crab, large strips of mackerel, or half a herring.

King ragworm, razor-fish, and clams are very effective in daylight, while lugworm is a useful bait at night. Spinning can be effective if there are plenty of jellyfish, or shoals of small fish or sand-eel about.

Bass are caught legering from groynes or piers, or the beach, but are not caught in shallow water if there is no cover for the angler.

In general, sandy beaches are best fished for bass at night, while rocky areas produce best results fished with crab bait in daylight. If the rocky patches cause problems with legers through fouling, try float-fishing with pike gear.

The bass has been called the 'salmon-bass', although there is absolutely no familial connection between the fish. It may be because the bass is very good to eat, or because it can give the lucky angler who hooks one a fine fight, or because of its silvery, salmon-like appearance when landed.

It may even be because sea-side landladies were rumoured to colour the flesh of the bass with cochineal to gull unsuspecting guests that they were being regaled with an expensive salmon, when there was really no need to dress up this magnificent meal.

beach casting – sea-fishing from a beach or rocks, using a suitable rod, reel, and weights, casting the bait out to where you think that there may be fish.

benthic – scientific term for fish that live on the sea-bed, either in shallow waters or in the deeper parts of the sea. The expression can also be used of fresh-water fish.

beetle – insect, usually with black wing-cases, that can be used for dapping for fish.

big game fishing – Angling for large specimen fish. Around Britain this has come to mean fishing for shark, with the occasional large halibut or skate getting in – there is some pressure to allow that conger is big-game.

Tunny in the North Sea used to be included, but with the over-fishing of the herring shoals, which they used to follow, tunny fishing has declined, although there is some commercial tunny fishing in the Bay of Biscay. If you are masochistic enough to wish to sail on the second roughest patch of water in the world, there are probably tunny to be caught.

Elsewhere in the world, of course, big game includes marlin, sailfish and swordfish.

billet – the young of the coalfish and pollack.

bite – the moment when a fish takes the bait into its mouth – indicated in various ways according to the type of fish and the method of fishing being used.

bite alarm – any audible device that indicates that the bait has been taken by a fish – these can be battery-powered, or a simple bell-on-a-clothes-peg type of contraption. Usually used at night, in other conditions of poor visibility, or when the angler fancies a nap!

bitterling – *rhodius sericus,* a small silvery, lustrous fish with an electric blue flash just in front of the tail, this is an introduction from Europe. This little fish, which only grows to 7cm (2.75in), is notable primarily for its breeding habit of laying its egg in the shell of a live swan mussel.

black bass – *micropterus dolomieu,* an introduction from America, where there are three species, the large-mouthed, the small-mouthed, and the spotted black bass.

Related to the perch, there seems to be no reason that these splendid fish should not acclimatise to British waters, but there is no sign of the species taking off in a big way here.

black bream – *sponyliosoma cantharus,* also known as the 'old wife'. Similar in shape to the freshwater bream, these marine fish are more solidly built, blue-black, with a large, spiny dorsal fin, and a forked tail.

They arrive on the south coast of England (probably from the Mediterranean) in spring, in large shoals, which feed together on shrimp, worms and crustacea. After about six weeks these shoals break up, and the fish disperse over a wider area, staying in the Channel until late August.

They are also found in smaller numbers off the western coast of Ireland, and even in the North Sea.

Black bream feed just off the bottom, and, fished with light tackle, using fish strips, cockles, worms, or shrimp as bait, will give good sport, as they fight far more strongly than their freshwater counterparts. All sea-bream are tasty, if a little bony for some. See also red bream, rays bream, pandora bream, and bogue.

black lug – a type of lugworm, not easily found as they burrow deep.

black nebs – localised name in Scotland for the sea trout.

black spot – a disease of freshwater fish, in particular the cyprinidae, caused by cercaria, a larva of the trematode worm.

The larva burrows just below the skin of the fish, causing a cyst. The disease does not appear to debilitate the fish and eventually disappears.

black trout – a colour variation of the brown trout, found in waters that have flowed through peaty country. Not actually black, just very dark in colour.

bleak – *alburnus alburnus,* also known as the willow-blade, a small silvery fish with a greenish back, another member of the cyprinid (carp) family.

The bleak grows to a maximum of 18cm (7in), usually seen at about 10cm (4in), and is primarily of interest to the angler as a makeweight in closely fought competitions, or caught for use as bait (live-baiting or dead-baiting).

Use lightweight tackle, small hooks (size 16-18) and small baits, such as maggots, bread paste, with a little ground-bait of similar form. Good sport can be had fly-fishing for these little fish, which, during the summer months, when other species are suffering from the torpor that overtakes them in hot weather, feed at the surface.

The fish is found mostly in running waters in the South East and Midlands of England, being seen but rarely in the South West and Wales or as far north as the Tees.

blennies – a family of small fish, the blennidae, that are of interest to the angler only as bait.

blood knot – (also known as the cruciform blood knot). A self-trapping knot most useful for tying slippery or mono-filament line of roughly similar sizes.

To tie, take the working ends of the lines to be tied and twist them around each other at least half a dozen times, then pass both working ends through the same central twist (in opposite directions).

Tighten each side of the knot by pulling on the standing parts, then the working ends. Trim the working ends.

If using to tie on droppers, one working end can be left long for this purpose. This knot is not recommended for wire or braided lines.

bloodworm – *chironomus,* the small larva of a midge, useable only on very fine tackle, with small hooks. The smallest of these worms are known as jokers, and are used as feed-bait in bait droppers.

blow lug – *see lugworm.*

blue shark – *prionace glauca,* as the name suggests, blue, with a white underside, this is the commonest shark found in British waters, usually in summer, west of Lyme Bay, round to the west coast of Ireland, and even, occasionally, off the west coast of Scotland in the warmer waters of the Gulf Stream.

Common around most of the south and south western seaboards of Europe, into the Mediterranean, as far east as Cyprus, the blue is rare anywhere in the English Channel to the east of the Isle of Wight.

The blue shark was probably the main instigator of the popularity of shark fishing in Britain. Not a great fighter once hooked, it still needs strong tackle, as although most of those caught are 1.2 metres to 1.5 metres (4 to 5ft) in length, they can grow to 7.5 metres (25ft).

They feed near the surface, mainly on herring, mackerel, and pilchard, which are the obvious baits.

boat – the types and sizes of boats from which angling is pursued are almost as numerous as the types and sizes of those that use them.

The prime requirements must be safety and seaworthiness, enough room in which to operate, and stability. If there is on board such equipment as an echo-sounder that will give an indication of fish below, and a R/T that enables your boatman (if you have one) to communicate with other skippers in order to find out what sport they are enjoying (some will tell, others never will), so much the better.

> If you are skippering the vessel yourself, and are going out of sight of land, please consider taking a navigation course before setting out.

boatman – the skipper or any helper on a hired boat.

WERE THEY FISHING?

The Owl and the Pussy-Cat went to sea
In a beautiful pea-green boat.
They took some honey,
and plenty of money,
Wrapped up in a five-pound note.
The Owl looked up at the stars above
And sang to a small guitar,
'Oh lovely Pussy!
Oh Pussy, my love,
What a lovely Pussy you are'.

(From The Owl and the Pussy-Cat – Edward Lear)

They used the stars for navigation!

---

boat rod – as sea-angling is a relatively young sport, the use of rods came about around the turn of this century, as a result of freshwater anglers accompanying fishermen to sea as guests aboard, using handlines as did their hosts.

These anglers knew that the rod gave a lot more scope in catching larger fish, more control over landing (or boating) them, so the sport of sea-angling began.

The first requirements for a boat rod were that it be short enough to manage aboard a boat in cramped circumstances, and that it be strong enough to cope with the large fish that could be expected. Rods of 1.5 to 1.8 metres (5 - 6ft), made of cane and/or split-cane predominated for many years, some with a steel rod or tube within to brace them.

With the advent of GRP (glass-fibre) and carbon fibre, and a better understanding of the dynamics, rods have improved immensely, as has their price.

A modern, hollow glass rod can be built to far more exacting standards, almost tailored to individual requirements.

By varying the taper of the mandrel on which it is built, and the thickness of the material at strategic points, the action can be influenced.

bogue – *boops boops,* a slender, smaller member of the sea-bream family, this fish is distinctively marked, with dark horizontal stripes on its yellow body.

Not so deep-bodied as the other bream, it feeds on the algae on rocks.

boilies – an artificial bait made by boiling together various ingredients (there are many recipes), and the keen experimenter can make up his own boilies with whatever he thinks the fish will like.

Boilies can be coloured to the individual's own taste, and are usually made into balls of varying sizes.

bonito – member of the tunny family, as is the mackerel, in shoals of which this fish is occasionally found, especially in the Irish Sea.

> Larger than the mackerel, without the striking stripey pattern, this fish is good eating, and should be barbecued or grilled in cutlets (flat slabs cut across the body), and served with plenty of lemon.

booby – artificial nymph that works oddly – it dips or dives when retrieved, and floats upwards when retrieval is stopped. Used for trout in deeper levels in cold conditions.

bootlace – colloquial name for a small eel.

bramble shark – *echinorhinus brucus,* so called because of the thorn-like projections on its back. Occasional in British waters.

bread – man's 'staff of life', useful as bait in several forms, such as flakes, cubes, crusts and paste, for many freshwater fish.

bread punch – a tube sharpened slightly at one end (somewhat like a leather punch), used to make a small roundel of bread as bait for roach, bream, etc.

breaking strain – the estimated (through thickness or diameter) or tested strength of a line when dry. This may be less when the line is wetted, or through use, or knotting. Often abbreviated to BS.

bream – *bramis brama,* the Common Bream, also known as the bronze bream, black bream, carp bream, etc., is a member of the carp (cyprinid) family. When young the bream is silver, darkening on the back with age to green-brown, brown, or slatey. coloured, even to black.

The flanks take on a bronze hue in older fish, and the belly darkens from white to buff. The back is humped, and the fish is deep in the body, the depth being about a third of the body length.

Bream are distinctive enough to make them easy to identify but hybrids (with the roach in England, and the rudd in Ireland) can lead to some confusion, and often the only sure way of distinguishing one from the other is to count the number of rays in the anal fin.

Bream have 23 to 29 rays, roach only 9 to 12, rudd 10 to 13. The roach/bream hybrid has 15 to 18, and the rudd/bream 15 to 18. Thus, if your catch has more than 12 rays, it is not a roach, if it has more than 13 it is not a rudd, and if it has less than 23 rays, it is not a bream. Which hybrid it is will depend upon location.

Bream move about the lake or river in shoals consisting mainly of fish about the same age and size, up to 50 fish patrolling in a regular pattern, feeding on worms, small crustacea, molluscs, and whatever they can find in the mud on the bottom of their habitat. This mud-grubbing releases decomposition gases which bubble to the surface, disturbing mud, something the experienced bream-fisherman watches for.

The best baits are worms, bread-based baits, maggots, nibs of sweetcorn, and freshwater mussels, and legend has it that anything containing or steeped in linseed oil is irresistible to the bream.

As the bream can grow up to 7kg (16lb), a strong rod will be necessary if pursuing specimen fish, although medium size bream can be taken on lighter equipment.

Float fishing, with the bait on (laying-up) or near the bottom, will get the best results, although legering is worth trying if the bottom is not so muddy that the weight or bait sink into the mud.

A good deal of ground-baiting is required to keep large shoals in the vicinity while the angler tempts them with his bait. Many pounds of ground bait can get used up, as these shoals can be up to fifty fish. Bread based or the commercially available ground bait are suitable.

Opinions differ as to whether the bream is worth eating. It has been compared to a mixture of sawdust and blotting paper, while another authority declares that its fat, tasty flesh makes it a valuable catch.

As to cooking methods, the common frying, grilling and baking will suffice, but a recipe found in a cookery book of 1655 suggests: ". . . and take the bream, stuffing a whole nutmeg into his mouth, and cast him, skipping, into the court-bouillon bubbling furiously . . ." although the prospect of cooking a fish from live will probably not appeal to everyone.

The silver bream is an independent genus, and is dealt with elsewhere.

brill – *scophthalmus rhombus,* smaller relative of the turbot, with which it can hybridise, this flatfish can be caught during the summer on mud or sand banks in shallow water, although in winter it migrates to deeper water.

Bottom-feeding, it takes sandeel, sprat, small crabs, etc, all of which make good baits for it.

> Excellent for the table, better flavoured than the turbot, larger specimens can go to 5kg (11lb). When cooking, be sure first to break the backbone in several places, as brill will tend to curl up if this is not done.

brown trout – *salmo trutta, see trout.*

bubble float – round, clear plastic float that imitates a bubble floating on the surface. It can also be filled to some degree with water to a level just before it sinks, making it useful for adding weight for casting.

bulge – the swell of water when a fish, particularly a trout, takes a fly just below the surface, rising without breaking the surface of the water.

bullhead – *cottus gobio*, an ugly little fish, also known as the miller's thumb, a member of the family cottidae, which are predominantly marine fish. With a flattened, frog-like head, seldom reaching more than 10cm (4in), these fish are of little interest except as bait.

bull huss – *see greater spotted dogfish.*

bull trout – *salmo eriox,* reputed variation of the sea trout or a marinised version of the brown trout, having similar colouration but differing in gill-cover and tail shape.

This may only be an older brown trout. Its name derives from its bullying activities among other trout and salmon, which leads one to think that it is not another genus, but merely a bad-tempered or psychotic trout.

bung – generic name for a pike float. The original 'bung' was an egg-shaped cork float.

burbot – *lota lota,* the only freshwater member of the cod family gadidae,is shaped rather like the ling, with a dorsal fin divided into two parts, anterior and posterior, and a long anal fin.

The anterior part of the dorsal fin is short, and the posterior part long. The mouth is cod-like, with a single barbel under the chin. Colour is greenish/brown, with darker shades and pale mottling, the underside being grey to yellow.

The burbot was often called the 'eel-pout' from its long body and wide mouth. A cold-loving fish that hunts smaller fish at night, its main spawning and feeding activity is during the winter, unlike most freshwater fish, and it does best in the parts of its range with a cold climate, reaching over a metre (3.5ft) and 22kg (50lb) in the Russian Onega Sea.

Limited to waters in the Eastern part of England from Durham down to East Anglia, the burbot is reputedly sought after as a tasty meal in Eastern Europe, where it is commercially fished, the liver, like that of the cod, being processed for its medically useful oil.

However, should you catch one in British waters, do not be tempted to mate it with chips.

They are now so rare here that they should be returned to the water, preferably in undamaged condition.

caddis fly – there are 5,000 species of caddis fly (trichoptera) worldwide, in 18 families.

The Northern caddis (limnephilidae), also known as the sedge fly, begins life on the river bottom, where, as a larva in a silken tube, it is prey in large numbers to trout.

However, as vast numbers are laid, myriads survive to become flies, which hatch on the stalks of sedge. These are also taken with great gusto by trout, particularly those that hatch during damp, warm evenings, the commonest being the Great Red Sedge, the Grannom (or 'Greentail'), the Silverhorns, the Silver Sedge, and the Cinnamon.

There are several artificial flies that are tied to resemble sedge flies.

carbon fibre – the material that is taking over from glass-fibre in the manufacture of fishing rods, used as the matrix in a resin moulding. Expensive, but very, very strong.

CHOOSE YOUR ROD CAREFULLY

See page 93 for a summary of rods and their uses.

Rods are no longer used for birching. They're better applied for catching fish.

THE GREAT CARP CATCHER

Of modern anglers, and writers on angling, none can be more famous than Dick Walker. Born in 1918, he wrote a weekly column for the *Angling Times* for more than thirty years, and the many thousands of words he wrote have been of immense instructional and inspirational value to anglers, from tyro to expert.

He caught many record fish, the magnificent 44lb carp taken in September 1952, dubbed Clarissa and kept until 1972 in the aquarium at London Zoo, probably the most famous.

A youngster reading any of Dick Walker's books or articles could rest assured that he never wrote about anything without experiencing if first – his hands-on research was second to none. He invented fishing methods, and articles of tackles (the Arlesey bomb springs to mind immediately).

His knowledge of angling was encyclopaedic, his writing style clear, simple, and instructive.

Richard Walker died in 1985, aged only 67. He was a dedicated naturalist, devoid of the venom that many anglers seem to have against other animals that compete for the same prey.

He defended otters and water voles against the calumnies heaped on them by less well-informed fishermen, and encouraged others to take a similar interest.

carp – although the carp family (Cyprinidae) includes many of the best-known coarse fish, such as barbel, bream, chub, dace, gudgeon, roach, rudd, tench, we will deal here with main members of the family, the common carp, crucian carp, leather carp, band carp, and mirror carp.

These fish may differ superficially, but are all (except for the crucian carp) members of the same genus, cyprinus carpio. The closely related crucian carp, *carassius carassius,* interbreeds readily with the others. Each will be dealt with separately.

Good to eat, resistant to disease, and a prolific breeder, cyprinus carpio in all its forms has been an economically important fish in the lower reaches of rivers and in ponds.

Originating in Europe (from the Caspian and Aral Seas westwards) and in the East from the Amur, north of Vladivostok round to Burma, it has been introduced around the rest of the world, probably reaching the British Isles in the fourteenth century.

Thermophilic, it does best in warm water areas, but grows rapidly almost anywhere, and, with the tench, was a staple in the stew-ponds of manors and monasteries, and, in the fifteenth and sixteenth centuries, in commercial warm-water fisheries.

In Britain, the advent of steam-driven transport during the industrial revolution meant that sea fish were more readily available, so farming of freshwater fish was neglected, and the introduced fish, now acclimatised to wild conditions, were left to themselves.

This did not occur on the Continent, and, as farming techniques improved, fish with tremendous growth rates were bred.

Introduction of these since the first World War has resulted, through interbreeding with the 'wild' varieties, in the production of large specimens that have come to be known as 'king carp'.

In middle and eastern Europe, the carp is revered as being fit for a banquet, and they are eaten with gusto in China.

The leather carp is farmed for food in Israel, and the roe of the carp has long been used in place of caviar by orthodox Jews, as their religion forbids the eating of any part of a fish without scales – into which definition the sturgeon, whence caviar is produced, falls.

From the angler's point of view, the carp can be found in rivers, but are more at home in lake or pond.

Usually bottom-dwellers, they also rise to the surface on warm, sunny days to bask, and they breed in the margins. They feed at temperatures between 14-18° C (56-69° F), at any time, day or night, when temperature and water conditions are right.

Distinguishing features include a hump-backed, oval-sectioned body, a long dorsal fin starting about halfway along the body, and four barbels, two on the upper lip, two at the corners of the small mouth.

Colour varies from grey-green to slate blue on the back, with the sides gold through to grey-green, with hints of pink, the belly ranging from yellow to orange.

Tough, crafty fish, carp, which commonly grow to 13.5kg (30lb) – the record on rod and line is over 23kg (51lb) – are fighting fish, and call for a heavily built rod with a good action all along its length.

cast – to throw a baited hook, line, and sinker using the leverage and spring in a rod, to the required place.

Also, the short length of line, usually of lower breaking strain than the rest of the line, to which the hook is tied.

casters – the chrysalis stage of the life-cycle of the fly, green-bottle, or blue-bottle.

They will sink in water only while they are a rich red hue, when they contain enough liquid, after which, when they have turned black, they float.

The red stage can be prolonged by preventing the loss of fluid, and keeping it cool, so, kept in a sealed plastic vacuum pack in the fridge, they can be kept in a state of arrested development far longer than the day or so that would normally be the case. However, they are still viable as hook-bait when black, as the weight of the hook and any shot will overcome the buoyancy.

Casters can be used as an addition to groundbait, or thrown loose into a swim (be sure to use casters of the same maturity, so that they do not float at different levels), and can be used as hook-bait on very fine hooks, size 16 to 18, to avoid smashing the thin shell.

> Unlike maggots, which are grabbed whole, the caster is usually sucked by fish, so it needs to be threaded up the shank of the hook. Bites are quick and light, so when you miss one, be sure to inspect your bait, or you will be fishing with an empty shell.

caterpillars – the larvae of various moths and butterflies, used especially during July and August in pools or rivers that are overhung by trees and bushes from which caterpillars are likely to hang, are deadly bait for trout.

If used when caterpillars are dropping from the trees, nature is doing your groundbaiting for you, and the larger trout will have driven the smaller fish away, in order to conserve the feast for themselves.

catfish – *siluris glanis,* also known as the wels or waller. This ugly fish has a wide mouth with long barbels around it, a smooth, scaleless, slimy skin, and was originally found in Middle European rivers such as the Rhine, Danube, and rivers flowing into the Baltic, Black, Caspian and Aral Seas, where it has been a commercially important fish.

Introduced into England at Woburn, they have spread to the Ouse and other East Anglian waters, where they have reached 15-16kg (33-36lb), although in European rivers they have grown to 80kg (180lb) or more. A much sought after quarry, the catfish demands heavy tackle, and will give a strong fight.

Its indiscriminate feeding habits suggest that it will take most baits, but live-baiting, dead-baiting, and legered worms, have proved best.

centre-pin reel – the traditional, old fashioned reel with a drum that revolves fore-and-aft in the line of the rod. Used for boat-fishing at sea, on piers and harbour walls, trotting a bait downstream, and fly-fishing.

cephalopods – octopuses, squid and cuttlefish.

chalk streams – rivers that originate on chalk hills, and by virtue of their cleanliness (through being filtered through chalk) offer an ideal medium for the growth of all the little organisms at the bottom of the food chain, at the top of which are the fish.

check – a ratchet on a fishing reel that can be disengaged to allow the spool to spin freely, or engaged to act as a drag on the line.

char – *salvelinus alpinus,* a cousin of the salmonid family, this colourful fish is biologically similar to, and follows habits similar to the salmon, breeding and spending its early years in the lower reaches of rivers, then maturing in the sea.

Widespread in the seas and rivers of Northern Europe, above 65° N, it is also found in the rivers of Canada, Greenland, Iceland, Norway, and Siberia. These fish can attain a length of a metre or more (3.5 feet), and a weight of 17 to 18kg (32lb), the size usually caught being around 450mm (1.5 ft) with a weight of about one kilo (2lb).

The quality of the flesh is akin to that of the sea trout. There are more than thirty forms of the genus that are solely fresh-water fish inhabiting the lakes of Ireland, Scotland, England, Norway, and the Alps.

The lakes of England, Scotland and Ireland on their own can boast at least fifteen species, each lake having its own outward variations, and in Lake Windermere there are two species that keep apart, even spawning at different times of the year.

These lake forms of the char are probably the descendants of the migratory form, landlocked at the end of the last Ice Age, and even now prefer deep, clean, cold waters.

Those in British lakes seldom grow very large, feeding on plankton and benthos, but in some European waters there are predatory forms that can reach 4 to 4.5kg (8-10lbs). Also, in Alpine lakes with poor food supplies there are pigmy forms - 100 to 150 mm (4-6 ins), 85 to 112g (3 to 4 ozs).

An introduction to Europe in the 1880s, the American brook trout, is in reality also a char, salvelinus fontinalis.

This beautiful fish is non-migratory, living in cool, clear brooks and mountain streams, where it can and does inter-breed with the brown trout. Attempts to acclimatise the migratory form, which, in the U.S.A. follows the river breeding and hatching, then the migratory habits of the rest of the salmonidae, have been unsuccessful.

chiromonoids – long-legged midges that inhabit reservoirs, known in the West Country as buzzers or racehorses, the pupae of which hang from the surface of the water just before they hatch. As large trout take these avidly, there are dozens of lures that try to simulate them in their myriad forms.

chub – *leuciscus cephalus,* a member of the carp family, and mostly a river fish, the chub has been introduced into lakes and ponds with some success, where it can grow larger than its river cousin.

Bronze/greenish-brown on the back, brassy on the flanks, fading to a yellowy-white on the belly, this is a chunky, tubby fish that is notoriously shy, and anyone approaching water to fish for chub is best advised to arrive quietly, keeping a low profile.

Chub feed on almost anything edible; nymphs, larvae, shrimps, crayfish, swan mussels, vegetable matter, fruit, and fry, even that of their own species. They are taken on a wide variety of baits, including berries, worms, and maggots, and they can even be tempted with artificial flies.

Izaak Walton recommended a large black slug as the ideal bait for chub.

When young, chub will shoal, mixing with roach, bream, rudd and dace. The chub will cross-breed with all of these, often leading to problems of identification. As they become older, they become more solitary.

Float or leger fishing will take chub, as will livebaiting with small fish such as minnows for the larger specimens, and the larger fish, over about 2kg (4.4lb) will give a good fight.

close season – coarse-fishermen have to desist from their sport from about the 14th of March until the 16th of June each year (there are local variations in these dates, usually with the effect of making the close season longer).

Game fishermen need to keep two sets of dates in mind – the salmon is off limits from 31st October until the 1st February, unless there are local byelaws, which take precedence, and the brown trout and sea-trout are out of season from 30th September until the 1st March. Rainbow trout are fair game the whole year round, and there is no close season for sea fishing.

Clyde fly – named for the river Clyde, these flies go against all the precepts of wet fly fishing, in that they have long, steeply-angled wings.

coachman fly – small trout fly, also used in fly-fishing for dace and roach.

coalfish – *pollachuis virens,* related to the cod, this fish has somewhat grey flesh (coley at the fishmongers) that whitens a little when cooked, but does not resemble the flesh of its cousin.

Usually caught around wrecks and rocky shores, this fish resembles the pollack, to which it is also related. They are distinguished by their lateral lines, that of the coalfish being a straight, white line, while the pollack's is black, and kinks up over the pectoral fin.

The coalfish also has a barbel under the lower jaw, which is itself less prominent that the pollack's. The coalfish prefers deeper levels than the pollack, and more brackish waters.

Strong tackle, fished between the wrecks or rocks and the surface, is recommended for this fast, predatory fish, which can grow up to 11.5kg (25lb).

coarse fishing – angling for any freshwater fish, excluding any members of the salmonidae family, (salmon, brown trout, rainbow trout, sea trout, etc.). The grayling, although a member of this family, is, for some reason, considered a coarse fish, though none the worse for this.

coch-y-bondhu – famous Welsh fly tied to resemble a red and black beetle found in the hills of Wales.

cockles – *cardium edule,* a small bivalve shellfish, much appreciated by humans, when they are boiled, and served with salt, pepper, and vinegar. The cockle uncooked is useful as bait for flatfish, or any other fish that inhabit the shallows and mudbanks where the cockle is found.

cod and codling – *gadus morhua*, the North Atlantic cod has been for many years the most important commercial fish in British waters, although it has declined of late through over-fishing.

Preferring colder waters, the cod migrates south in the winter as far as the south west coast of England, returning north in the summer, entering the shallows to spawn at varying times of the year, depending on local conditions.

Distinguished from the pollack by having a white lateral line, (which curves in the same way as the pollack's, which is dark), and a receding lower jaw, which has a barbel under the lower lip. As in most fish, colouration varies, but the predominant version is grey-green back and flanks, with brown spots, and a white belly. The lateral line is, as mentioned, white, and curves over the pectoral fins.

Heavy tackle is called for if big cod are expected – they can grow to 18-22kg (40-50lb) – and lots of line as they prefer deep water (30 to 40 fathoms). Fish under 2.7kg (6lb) are referred to as codling.

Although mostly caught from boats, cod are also landed by beach-casters, and, with their huge mouths, can take a wide variety of baits.

The usual size of fish taken is about 4.5kg (10lb), whether beach or boat fishing, and the record boat-caught fish is just over 23kg (50lb). Commercially caught fish of up to 90kg (200lb) are not uncommon.

> Apart from its value as food, the cod is important for the oil in its liver, which is rich in vitamins and used in many medicines.

coffin lead – a weight used for legering, in the shape of a rectangle with the corners cut off, nowadays not usually made of lead, but of a non-toxic metal. Available in straight-through form (with a hole drilled through from end to end for the line to pass through), or swivelled (having a swivel at each end with eyes to which the line is tied).

Colorado spoon – a triple-hooked spinning spoon with vanes at the front end.

conger eel – *conger conger,* the largest of the eels, a fish of many legends, the conger is unmistakable, unlike any other fish. Far larger than any common eel, with massive jaws, formidable teeth, and a powerful, muscular body, they reach well over 45kg (100lb).

They prefer warmer waters, and inshore fish may move into deeper waters during the winter, but they are not migratory until the urge comes on them to spawn, when they follow the age-old eel routes to the Sargasso Sea.

All the enormous congers caught have been female, the largest males caught being about 16kg (35lb).

Distribution is wide, spawning taking place in the depths of the ocean, as far down as 2000 fathoms (3660m), and the bathypelagic eggs float in the depths (it seems that the eggs need the great pressures found at depth to mature), on currents that take them as far north as the southern parts of Scandinavia, as far south as the coast of equatorial Africa, and all over the Mediterranean Sea.

Related species are found in warm waters all over the world. It would seem that the larger the fish, the deeper it lives, but some huge specimens have been caught inshore.

Most harbours and inshore wrecks seem to have congers of reputed vast dimensions, that have smashed dozens of anglers' tackle.

Conger live on fish, lobster, crab, octopus, and cuttlefish, and tend to live in holes, caves and reefs, or wrecks close to good food supplies.

The fish is found all around the British Isles, but less so in northern and eastern waters, the largest being caught in the south, south west, Wales, and Ireland.

Heavy tackle is needed, as the fish put up a terrific fight when near the surface, as, unlike other deepwater fish that suffer from the bends on coming up from the depths, they have a way of equalising pressure by releasing air from their bodies as they rise. Once they are landed, great care must be taken to avoid injury from the powerful jaws and sharp teeth of a lively, thrashing eel.

A suitable box or well in the boat would be of use, or a covering such as a sack will quieten a conger.

> Moderate sized conger are good eating, and are best smoked. If you catch a really big specimen, donate it to some institution, as it will take up all the room in your freezer.

controller – a weighted float, used primarily in carp fishing, the added weight being an aid to casting.

corkwing wrasse – *crenilabrus melops,* a small member of the wrasse family, growing only up to 23cm (9in). Variable in colouration, a distinguishing feature is the dark spot in the wrist just in front of the caudal fin (tail).

Usually brightly coloured, the corkwing has a blue or green streak around and under the jaws. Found, like the other wrasse, on the south and southwest coasts of England and Ireland.

> **cormorant** – large sea-bird that has lately, because of the depredations on marine fish stocks by the fishing industry, moved inland, and made inroads on the coarse- and game-fisherman's preserves.
>
> Culling has taken place, and many fisheries have reported that fewer cormorants are being seen each year.

> **corrosion** – the gas upon which life on Earth depends, oxygen, is among the most corrosive substances in the universe, and metals that come into contact with water – especially salt water – are prone to some attack from rust or other surface corrosion.
>
> Maintenance in the form of drying and oiling or greasing reels, rod-rings and other metal equipment is essential. Modern lines are fairly maintenance-free, whereas old-fashioned lines needed drying, and in some cases, oiling. Some fly lines, with modern plastic coatings (polyvinyl chloride or PVC) leach out their plasticizer, and need lubrication with a special lubricant.

crab – *decapoda cancer,* exo-skeletal crustacean with ten legs, sometimes a nuisance, sometimes very useful. By their very nature, bottom feeders, crabs are a nuisance when, in their normal foraging, they pick up a bait on a legered hook, and get snarled up in the line, causing unbelievable tangles. However, if the crab is of the edible variety, the angler has his meal, anyway.

Spider crabs, although canned in the Far East at Khamchatka, seem to have very little appeal when you are trying to untie a bird's nest with cold, wet hands, on a heaving boat.

As bait, small crabs take a variety of fish, bass, brill, coalfish, dogfish, skate, and turbot.

Peelers (small crabs that are just about to shed their carapaces as part of the growing process), and softbacks (those that have just moulted the carapace) are usually preferred as bait, but hardshells are just as readily taken by larger fish.

The crabs, which can readily be found in rockpools, under wet seaweed, or under rocks at low tide, are usually hooked through the rear end of the shell (after being killed, of course), or hooked on to a small elastic band around the animal. Smaller fish such as dabs or flounders will take hooks baited with part of a small crab.

Hermit crabs, which use empty whelk shells as their homes because they do not form carapaces of their own, are easily found, and are a natural bait taken by a wide variety of bottom feeding fish.

crab line – short length of braided line, wound on a wooden or plastic frame, usually equipped with weights and a paternoster, sold at sea-side resorts to small boys, for fishing off the pier or harbour wall.

Crabtree, Mr – a strip-cartoon character created by Bernard Venables, each strip giving advice (as to a small boy) about aspects of angling. This strip appeared throughout the 1940s, 50s, and 60s, and re-appeared on television in the mid-1990s.

crayfish – the only crayfish native to Britain is the white-footed, *autropotomobius pallipes,* found all over, but preferring lime- or chalk-rich rivers and streams (it uses the lime to build up its shell), with lots of rocks, or nooks and crannies.

Cultivated all over the Continent as a table delicacy – the red footed crayfish, *astacus astacus,* is the variety found here – it has been neglected in Britain, as the white-footed does not grow big enough to make it attractive. However, they are good to eat, as many trout would agree, having fallen victim to a tail used as bait.

creeper – the larva of the stone-fly. Easily found under stones in April and May when they leave the water to transmogrify themselves into flies, they make excellent bait for many coarse fish.

crucian carp – *carassius carassius,* a member of the cyprinidae family, less sought after than the common carp because it is generally smaller – growing to about 2kg (4.4lb). The main recognition point when comparing the crucian with the common carp is the lack of barbels around the mouth.

In shape it generally resembles the common bream. Preferring slow-moving rivers and streams with pools and secondary branches, it is not oxygen demanding, and can live in fairly murky water.

An introduced fish, (intended as a decorative addition to domestic ponds) originating in Eastern Europe, it is now to be found as far north as the arctic Ocean margins, and as far east as the Caspian Sea. In common with another cyprinid, the tench, it can survive extreme drought conditions by living buried in mud when a pond dries out.

The crucian carp can provide good sport if fished with light, float tackle, using maggots or bread baits, fished on the bottom. It is related more closely to the goldfish, *carassius auratus auratus.*

cuckoo wrasse – *labrus mixtus,* a small red fish with, in the male, bright blue stripes. Grows to about 30 cm (12in). Found around the southwest coast of England, and off the coasts of Ireland.

cuttle-fish – *sepia officinalis,* the common cuttle-fish grows to about 30cm (12in) long. It has ten tentacles, and a fan-like fin all around its body, which it undulates when swimming. Good as bait, either whole or cut into pieces. Conger, bass, coalfish, etc. will fall to this bait.

cuttyhunk – old-fashioned line made of wound linen, named for the island where it was introduced, Cuttyhunk Island, Massachusetts.

dab – *limanda limanda,* a small flatfish that prefers inshore sand-, mud- or gravel-banks, where it lives on worms and crustacea.

Any confusion over identification can be dispersed by looking at the lateral line, which in the dab goes above the pectoral fin in a sharp peaked line, rather like a line on a graph, rather than the curve of the other flatfish. Growing to a maximum of about 1kg (2.2lb), it is good eating, particularly when very fresh, tasting similar to plaice.

Beach-casting, pier fishing, or boat-fishing will all produce results, using a paternoster carrying 2 or 3 worms – lugworm, ragworm – or mussel or shrimp. Some authorities insist that the bait should not be left lying around, but made more interesting by being moved a few inches occasionally.

When fishing for dab, take a disgorger, as they are renowned for taking the bait and hook deep into the mouth.

CULINARY GUIDANCE

Steamed Fish

Wash, scale and prepare the fish. Cover it with some greaseproof paper and place in the steamer. Allow about 20 minutes per kilo.

If you have thin fillets, just steam them between two plates with a little milk added.

Serve with a garnish of parsley and a sauce of your choice.

dace – *leuciscus leuciscus,* a slender, silvery fish of the cyprinidae family, similar to the chub, to which it is related, and with which it hybridises, the main point of differentiation being the anal and dorsal fins, which are convex in the chub, concave in the dace.

Greenish/brown on the back, the fins are yellowish to pink.

Like most members of the carp family, dace move in shoals, usually in the shallows of fast-flowing clean water, although they can be found in slow-flowing or still waters.

Dace feed on flies, larvae, snails, worms, and silkweed, but the most effective bait for them is the maggot. They will also take worms, caterpillars, caddis grubs, freshwater shrimp, bread paste, bread flake or crust, and hempseed.

Fine tackle and a small hook (size 18-20), a slim float, and good reflexes are required, as this is a cautious, fast fish that snatches at food.

Legering on the bottom will often catch the larger fish, but the bait must move about a bit. Dace are not very big fish, the largest barely reaching 0.5kg (1lb).

Good sport can be had in the summer by dry fly fishing when they are surface feeding on natural flies.

daddy longlegs – a dry fly tied to simulate the crane fly. It should be used, as with all lures made to simulate the action of all land-borne insects that get blown into or fall into the water – that is, they do not struggle, but rather quickly give up, and lie still. Such dry flies should be cast to the position wanted, and left to lie there.

Dark Olive Quill – an artificial fly.

Dark Spanish Needle – an artificial fly.

dap, dapping – also called dibbling, a delicate manner of fishing for surface feeding fish by lowering a baited hook onto the surface.

As the fish would be able to see the angler, it pre-supposes some method of concealment or camouflage. Frequently used with live insects such as grasshoppers or woodlice.

daphnia – the 'water flea'. Actually, not a flea or an insect, but a minute freshwater crustacean, which make up a large part of the diet of young trout, and upon which they love to feed.

day fly – a group of flies that are short-lived in their mature stage – not all for just a day, but some for not much more. Their main life is lived as a nymph, under water, then they surface, shed a skin, becoming a dun, (they are vulnerable during this operation), then shedding a further skin to become a spinner, or mature fly.

At the end of the life-cycle they lay their eggs, and lie, exhausted and dying, on the surface of the water. Artificial flies representing any of these stages and transitions will catch trout.

dead-baiting – using a small dead fish, either legered, or trotted in order to simulate a live, if somewhat sick, fish.

If being legered, the bait can be hooked through the lip, and, with a suitable bait, fished downstream in fast running water, wobbling in the stream, again simulating a live, distressed fish.

Hook through the body, using a baiting needle, with a treble hook, either with the hooks at the tail end, or with the fish facing the hooks. With the hooks at the tail, the sink and draw method is used, the bait being drawn up to the surface, then allowed to sink.

This is repeated, yet again simulating a dying fish – a weight in the fish's mouth helps in this, making it dive head first, rather than sink level. Don't give up on this until the bait is really close to the bank, as many fish will follow, then strike when the quarry is approaching the 'safety' of the bank.

dead-bait flight – two sets of treble hooks are whipped together in tandem (one behind the other), and a bait needle, with or without spinning vanes, is threaded on the cast above them. A dead-bait is then mounted on this rig, with the needle pushed though the fish's mouth, and the hooks stuck into its flanks.

The dead-bait will wobble through the water in a convincing manner. If vanes are used, it will spin, and a swivel will be necessary.

Deal yellow-tail – a type of lugworm that leaves a yellow stain on the skin if handled.

> **Decca Navigator** – an electronic navigation device that fixes a vessel's position by receiving signals from shore stations – a useful way of finding your way back to that wreck, or a good reef.

deep diver – type of plug with a diving vane so angled that it causes the plug to dive steeply and deeply.

> **deep-sea fishing** – fishing off-shore, usually further out than is safe in a dinghy, in a somewhat larger boat.

As a wide range of gear is required to get the most out of this sport, a good way of finding out if you like it is to take advantage of one of the trips offered at sea-side resorts. Rods and tackle are provided, and the boats have to be registered by the Board of Trade, and must carry all the necessary safety and rescue gear.

If you decide that you like it, then buy the gear necessary for the type of fishing you prefer.

You may carry on deep-sea fishing from chartered or hired-by-the-hour boats for the rest of your life, in which case you will soon become familiar with the vagaries and talents of individual skippers, who may or may not supply bait, who may or may not know the best marks, some of whom can smell a school of fish ten fathoms down, and some of whom will not venture out of the harbour if the waves are more than two feet high.

If you are wealthy, or adventurous, you may decide to buy your own boat, in which case you will have the responsibility of maintaining, navigating, steering, and supplying your own bait.

Be prepared for sea-sickness, or take the pills. Have a good supply of traces and weights organised beforehand – tying on hooks in a pitching, rolling boat with cold, wet hands, is no joke.

Also, take plenty of bait – it is better to throw away excess ragworm than run out after a couple of hours, having motored out twenty miles against a strong wind.

> Lastly, take plenty of warm and/or waterproof clothing as you can always take it off if you become unbearably hot, but you cannot put more on if you left it at home!

demersal – living on or near the bottom.

demon – an artificial lure made from feather strips and tinsel, intended to represent a small fish.

Devon minnow – a small, streamlined spinning lure, based upon a tube, through which the line is passed, to end in a treble hook.

A swivel above the body of the minnow helps keep the line from twisting, and there are two vanes at the front end that act like a screw or propeller, spinning the body – the hooks, not being fixed to the body, remain stationary. The body can be of different materials – metal, which will not need any weights to keep it down in the water; plastic, which acts more naturally, but needs weight on the line in front of it; wood, as for plastic; and quill, useful as a light summer spinner.

In varying sizes, a good general purpose spinner for trout, salmon, pike – in fact, any predatory fish.

dibbling – see 'dapping'.

dinghy – small boat propelled by oars, outboard engine, or sails.

We will ignore the use of sail-power here, as they only get in the way of the rods – unless, of course, you happen to be a dinghy sailor who keeps a crab line aboard while away the idle hour whilst becalmed!

The dinghy can get you to places that a larger boat with a deep draught cannot reach, and of which a beach-caster can only dream. Always carry safety gear – flares, fresh water, emergency food (you never know when that calm day might change, even if you did listen to the weather forecast).

Wear a buoyancy aid (even a good swimmer is in trouble if he knocks his head as he falls overboard), and inform someone of the area of your trip and estimated time of return, even if you are in familiar waters, and don't intend to go out of sight of land – fogs and mists are no respecters of persons, nor are offshore

Whether using oars or an outboard, trolling or whiffing is probably the best use to which a dinghy can be put, but it is inadvisable to do this while alone – shipping oars or controlling an outboard whilst trying to reel in that "big 'un" calls for more than one pair of hands.

dip minnow – see drop minnow.

dipping – see 'dapping'.

diseases – see under Spring Viraemia, Trichodina, Ulcerative Dermal Necrosis, and sea lice.

disgorger – in angling, to disgorge means to remove the hook from the mouth of the fish.

As the hook can often be deep in the animal's mouth, even into the throat, some device is often necessary. There are many types, from a simple tube with a slot that slides down the line to the hook, to long-nosed pliers, with many permutations between.

"You pays your money, and you takes your choice!"

diving vanes – a lip at the front of some plugs that causes them to dive when pulled through the water. Some are adjustable for angle, to vary the depths to which they will dive.

dock grubs, docken grubers – the white grub of a small beetle that eats the roots of the common dock plant. Easy to dig out, these were once very popular bait, and are free!

dogfish – members of the shark family. *See greater spotted dogfish, lesser spotted dogfish, and spur dogfish.*

---

dog food – a useful additive to many baits, or even used on its own.

---

double grinner knot – when tying knots in fly lines, a knot that will not snag on the rod-rings is needed. The double grinner is used to tie the line to the leader.

It is formed by twisting the two parts together about six or eight times, then looping the working parts of each strand back to the middle of the twist, and threading it several times around the original twist, in the same direction, under the looped part. This, when pulled tight, with the working parts snipped flush, gives a smooth knot that will not impede the passage of the line.

double handed casting – when using a beach-caster or a heavy-duty spinning rod, it can be necessary to cast using two hands.

double-haul cast – a way of making a really long cast when using a shooting line.

Begin with all of the belly and back taper of the shooting head beyond the rod tip, with the body weight on the forward foot, which should be the opposite to the hand holding the rod.

The rod is swung back overhead as the free hand pulls hard down on the line. When the rod reaches its furthest back point of travel, the free hand is slid up to the first ring to repeat the pull on the line as the rod is flicked forward.

As the rod is stopped at the furthest forward point of travel, the line held by the free hand is let go, and the point of the rod lowered gently to ensure a soft landing of the line on the water, rather than a whip-lash effect.

double-rubber – a float used with a small rubber band at each end to hold the line.

double-tapered lines – fly lines are tapered in order to make the part that lays on the water lighter. Double-taper lines (designated DT) are tapered for the last 3-3.6m (10-12ft) at each end so that when one end is worn, the line can be reversed on the reel, and the other end used.

dough – flour and water mixed to form a squidgy paste or dough, to which can be added flavourings such as salmon paste, or any potted fish or meat sandwich spread. Crucian carp are suckers for this paste with a custard powder admix.

dough bobbin – a ·lump of dough squeezed on to the line between the reel and the first rod-ring to act as a bite indicator when legering.

drag – the wake left by an unnaturally presented dry fly, caused by moving it across or against the current, which will not fool even the most stupid trout. Also, a clutch on a fishing reel, *see star drag*. Also, to use the thumb or a finger to act as a brake on a reel.

dragonfly – pretty to watch as you sit by a river on a summer's evening, the dragonfly family libellula can be responsible for a dearth of fish to catch, as the larvae of this fly can demolish a trout populace by eating vast numbers at the alevin stage, also wreaking havoc amongst other insects.

drift fishing – fishing over wrecks, allowing the boat to drift, trailing the lines over the side away from which the boat is moving (otherwise the lines will trail under the hull).
Speed of drift can be controlled by the use of a drogue and/or sea-anchor.

drift line – trailing a weighted line from a boat, so that the tackle streams out in the current, just off the bottom.

drilled bullet – a round weight with a hole drilled through it, used in situations where a rolling leger is required. The line is passed through the weight, and shots are pinched on either side of it to limit its movement up and down the line.

drip-feed – a method of gradually ground-baiting a small area by hanging a container with holes in the bottom and/or sides, whence maggots can wriggle, to fall a few at a time into the water, keeping fish interested in the area.

drogue – a conical bag made of canvas or plastic, trailed on a rope from the stern of a vessel to control directional stability or speed of drift. *See also sea-anchor.*

drop minnow – method of dead-baiting – in which a minnow has a slim straight-through weight pushed inside it, and the line threaded through with a needle, a hook being tied on the end. It is then fished with the sink-and-draw method, under banks, in deep pools, anywhere a large trout might lay.

drop net – a landing net on a rope, used for landing fish when angling from a pier, groyne, or harbour wall, where a gaff or an ordinary net on a pole will not reach.

dropper – extra flies tied to the main cast on short casts when wet fly fishing, the main fly being called the point fly.

dropper knot – the knot used for tying a wet fly 'dropper' to a cast. First tie a blood knot in the cast, then tie on the dropper above this with an overhand knot around the cast, then take the dropper once around the cast, and pass it through its own loop in a half-hitch.

dry fly – an imitation fly tied to resemble or represent a natural fly or any other insect, usually waterproofed or treated with a floatant, and fished to float on the surface. Used on lakes or slow-flowing rivers.

dun – a larval stage in the development of a mayfly (ephemeridae) between hatching and shedding its skin and becoming a mature fly or spinner.

Dunkeld fly – an artificial fly.

echo-sounder – electronic device that consists of a transducer fitted under the hull which sends out a sound signal, and on receiving the return, which has bounced back off the sea-bed and/or any solid object in its path, translates that signal into a read-out on a cathode ray tube (like a small television screen), or, on some older types, a pen-line on a paper roll.

Thus, a representation of the contours of the sea-bed, and any wrecks or reefs that may harbour fish can be seen, as can shadowy traces that denote shoals of fish.

Seemingly easy to operate, these instruments take some experience to interpret, so either leave them to experienced skippers, or cut your teeth on open waters before trying them inshore.

eel – *anguilla anguilla,* long, slender, snake-like fish with a dorsal fin that extends from about one third of the way along the body to join the anal fin to form the tail, the anal fin having started about halfway along the body.

The eel appears scaleless – in fact it has tiny scales that are embedded in the skin. It is only during the last seventy or so years that we have come to any sort of understanding of the eel's life-cycle, and even now some parts are still clouded in mystery.

We know that spawning takes place in the Sargasso Sea, at great depth, seemingly needing the great pressure to mature into a sort of larva, and that the tiny transparent larvae are wafted towards Europe by the Gulf Stream.

By the time they reach Northern waters they have developed into elvers, a few inches long, and they disperse into rivers, interlinked waterways, and, via drainage ditches and wet grassland, into landlocked lakes. They grow to a good size – up to 2kg (4.4lb) is common enough, and fish of 5 to 7kg (11 to 16lb) have been known – and to a good age, although just how old is still open to conjecture, but it is probably about ten years.

Neither is it known what triggers the spawning urge that drives them down to the sea, in an effort to reach the Sargasso again, but it is thought that none of the European eels ever reach their goal, and that all the new stock that is born each year is from eels that have inhabited the eastern American seaboard. Furthermore, there is no evidence that the eel survives the spawning experience.

Eels are not hard to catch – indeed, they often jump on the hook while the angler is assiduously trying for something else – but the really large ones do seem to be a bit more canny than more moderate sized specimens.

Eels of over 2kg (4.4lb) have been found in reservoir sumps, when nothing like that size has been caught in the locality. If you are out specifically for eel, use a strong trace – wire, or stout nylon monofil – as they have sharp teeth, and have a wet cloth ready, as they are very slimy and difficult to hold when removing the hook.

eel *(continued)*

Be sure, also, to use one or more swivels in the tackle, as one trick of these fish is to rotate. Many anglers use a hook without a barb, to facilitate removal.

Best baits are lobworm, maggots, any meat or offal, and if you are trying for the larger specimens, dead-baiting with part of a fish or a whole small fish.

In East Anglia, babbing or bobbing is a sporting method of eel-fishing much favoured. Remember, the eel is very supple, can wind itself around underwater projections, and can swim backwards powerfully, so do not give him the respect you offer other fish – do not play him, just get him out of the water as quickly as you can, and into a suitable receptacle, the tangle an eel can make of your tackle has to be seen to be believed.

They make good eating, although some people are put off by the sliminess, and the difficulty there seems to be over killing them. Jellied (boiled, and allowed to cool in its own liquor), poached with a parsley sauce, served with mashed potatoes, or hot smoked – one of the tastiest of fish!

eel-grass – *zostera marina,* a thin weed once found all around the coasts of Britain, that had declined almost to the point of extinction, but is now returning. A good feeding ground for many fish.

elderberry – small blue-black fruit of the elder bush, which will take roach and chub, particularly if there is an elder overhanging the stream or lake. Fish them on a small hook (16 to 18) near to the bush.

electronic bite indicator – also known as bite alarms, these are small battery operated electronic circuits that depend upon the movement of the line when it is taken by the fish to sound a buzzer, although they can be rigged to turn on a small bulb.

Mostly used for night-fishing for carp, although they have been seen in use during the day, presumably by night-shift workers who wish to continue their sport without losing too much sleep!

elvers – after being spawned in the depths of the Atlantic, and being wafted north northeast by the Gulf Stream, the tiny eel larvae (leptocephalus) reach the coastal waters of Europe, and, having grown to about 8cm (3in) in length, in springtime start to ascend the rivers.

By this time they have metamorphosed into elvers, and opinion is divided about which elvers actually make this run, the theory that only the females go inland, with the males staying in the estuaries and coastal waters, holding sway at the moment.

Whether this sexual differentiation is part of the spawning urge that takes them out to sea later is problematical.

Elvers are trapped in large numbers on their way up-river. On the Severn it has become a ritual, with much being made of the gastronomic delight of elvers in local hostelries.

The taking of thousands of immature fish in the lower reaches of rivers would normally seem ecologically unsound, but eels are a great nuisance in trout waters, taking the alevin, and depriving the larger trout of food, and if the thousands that are culled were left to survive, it would seem that eel would be the only thing for which we could angle.

The elver is taken as food by many fish, so while it would be pointless to use one elver among many thousands when they are running, a few dozen caught at this time and preserved or frozen would make good bait for a future occasion.

entomology – the science of insects. Of interest to anglers insofar as the fly-fisherman needs to know something of the habits of the flies and other bugs he is trying to simulate, although it is now generally agreed that the efforts of Victorian anglers to imitate flies exactly was over-weening and unnecessary, and the emphasis is now on the suggestion of a fly, rather than its exact copying.

ephemera – the genus of insect whose life-span is very short, such as the may-fly.

ephemerid – an insect of the may-fly family. The ephemereidae (the name means 'a day on the wing') may only live as flies for one day, but they have spent a couple of years or more developing underwater, in a complex life-cycle, during which they are part of the food-chain of many aquatic life-forms.

The part that interests fishermen is the time the larvae spend floating to the surface to metamorphose into the fly. It is then that trout become interested in them, and which the wet fly is supposed to emulate.

AN OPEN LETTER

To Dr. Samuel Johnson (1709-1784)

Dear Dr. Johnson

You are regarded by many as the greatest man of letters England has produced.

Your dictionary, published in 1755, despite a rejection by Lord Chesterfield, is the basis upon which all our present dictionaries and encyclopaedia are produced.

You are the doyen of dictionary-compilers! Furthermore, your brilliant 'put-downs' (that's not in *your* dictionary, by the way) are recorded and remembered.

However, your comment about fly-fishing is too much for any self-respecting fish to swallow.

In his 'Instructions to Young Sportsmen' (1859), page 197, Hawker has attributed to you the following offensive lines: "Fly-fishing may be a pleasant amusement; but angling or float fishing I can only compare to a stick and a string, with a worm at one end and a fool at the other."

Now, Sir, over 200 years later, would you accept that times have changed?

First, would you agree that worms are only occasionally used? Second, would you agree that rods have replaced sticks? Third, would you agree that not all fishermen are fools?

Have you ever heard of Ernest Hemingway? No fool, he!

Reply at your leisure, Sir.

Yours piscatorially

The Editor

estuary fishing – the estuary, the place where the river flows into the sea, where, as can be expected, there is a mixture of conditions and environments.

The mixture differs from river to river, according, mainly, to the size of the river, the terrain around the river, the amount of water coming down the river, and the speed of that water. Thus, different conditions will prevail at the estuary of a river descending rapidly, hemmed in by a mountainous or hilly coastline, that is unable to spread itself, from those in a wide, meandering river slowly snaking across lowland plains, spreading out into a delta at its mouth.

The key to understanding estuary fishing lies in realising that here is the confluence of fresh and salt water, and the power of the body of water moving down a river should not be underestimated.

Sailors of the square-riggers that first explored the eastern seaboard of the Americas were amazed to find that they could lower a bucket over the side and draw up drinkable fresh water out of sight of land – the Amazon and the Orinoco are still flowing some miles out to sea! So, your fishing will be different in different estuaries.

Where a slow-moving, wide river meets the sea, the area probably has mud or sandbanks. Mud flats that are exposed at low tide make excellent bait-gathering ground, and flounder, mullet, eels, and garfish and, in the rivers they frequent, sea-trout will be found in the shallow, food-rich, brackish waters, waiting for food to be brought to them by the tide.

Beach-casting with relatively light tackle will give good sport in these conditions.

Out in the middle of the estuary, the stronger, fish such as bass, where the tidal flow will be, dislodge the lugworm, and ragworm, but you will need a small boat to fish here.

Where the estuary widens and the freshwater flow lessens, the tidal flow dominates, and the water takes on greater salinity. Here the more truly marine species (cod, plaice, conger etc) will be found, and a larger boat, with a substantial anchor would be advantageous.

In many estuaries a sandbar, built up by the action of tide and river-flow, will run right across, and, apart from being a danger to navigation, will be to the benefit of the angler, as here mackerel will abound.

These conditions prevail in all estuaries, but the shape of them depends entirely upon the flow and power of the river.

evening rise – that time of the evening after a summer's day when the cooling of the water, the return of flies to the water to lay their eggs, and the hatching of other flies combine to cause trout to rise to the surface to feed. This short time is the fly-fisher's paradise.

false-cast – when fly-fishing, in order to cast further than the amount of line that is thrown by the first cast, the rod is pulled back before the line hits the water, and the casting action repeated, as often as necessary, letting more line out with each false-cast until there is enough line out to reach the spot required.

feathers, feathering – several sea-fish are attracted to lures made of, or decorated with feathers, mackerel being the best-known, while cod, pollack, coalfish, and ling will also fall for such lures.

February Red fly – a rare stone-fly that occurs, when found, in the early part of the year.

ferox trout – a variation of the trout found in deep Scottish lochs.

ferrule – the ends of the sections of a fishing-rod, designed to push into each other.

> **fibre-glass rods** – fishing rods were originally made of whatever could be found in the hedgerow, and when the sport developed, the importation of bamboo made the split-cane rod possible.
>
> These held sway until the 1960s, when glass re-inforced plastic (GRP) was developed. This material, which consists of fine threads of glass in a resin matrix, is used to build boats, cars, telephone boxes, any number of everyday objects.
>
> The advantages of its use in fishing rods are its tensile strength, elasticity, flexibility, and freedom from attack by rot-producing organisms. Early glass-fibre rods were of solid construction, and had a somewhat 'dead' feel, but modern rods are hollow, with a lot more responsiveness.

figure-of-eight knot – not the well-known knot that yachtsmen use as a stopper, but a non-slip knot used to attach a fly-line to a looped leader. It is made by passing the working end of the fly-line up through the loop, taking it round underneath the loop, then bringing it up and through its original entry as in a sheet bend.

However, instead of stopping there, the working end is then brought round again and taken back under the same part.

figure-of-eight retrieve – a method of bundling the retrieved line in the hand, rather than having loops of it trailing around the feet. The line is pulled back with the index and little fingers alternately, and stored in the crook of the thumb.

fingerling – another name for a trout parr.

fining – the process whereby matter suspended in a liquid gradually falls to the bottom, leaving the liquid clear. When soil particles and other detritus falls to the bottom in a flooded river, fish start to feed again after the rigours of the flood.

finnock – one of the several local names for the young sea-trout.

> **first aid** – a knowledge of first aid is useful for everybody, but the obvious parts of it essential for the angler are procedures for removing hooks stuck into various parts of the anatomy (the angler's own, and bystanders whom he has hooked), cuts, and resuscitation following immersion in water for those unfortunate enough to fall in, up to and including artificial respiration, and treatment for hypothermia.

fishery – any stretch of water containing fish, specifically denoted as such, stocked for angling, that would not ordinarily be recognised as such – namely, reservoirs, and parts of lakes and lochs set aside for the purpose in tourist areas.

fish farming – fish have been farmed for centuries – carp and such in stew-ponds before transport improved enough to make marine fish viable in the depths of the country – and, in the nineteenth century, brown trout were reared for re-stocking purposes when game fishing became fashionable with the gentry.

Nowadays the re-stocking still goes on, but most fish-farming is geared to the restaurant table, or the supermarket deep-freeze, and the pre-dominant fish used is the American rainbow trout, which has the advantage over the brown in growth rate and conversion of food.

Many reservoirs are stocked with these fish, which do well when the reservoir is new, and food is plentiful, but drop back as the food becomes used up and competition from other species increases.

A recent trend has been for fish that have been 'artificially grown' to large sizes by being intensively fed in virtual captivity, then released for anglers to catch. These somewhat tame fish do not offer the sport to be expected from wild fish, or farmed fish that have been feral for a season or two.

> **fishing club** – local groups found all over the country, some calling themselves 'Angling Societies', but all existing for the same reasons – to promote the sport in the area, control fishing rights on local waters, and generally socialise in a fishy way.

fixed leger – a simple, sensitive method of legering that entails the use of a single large shot fixed a couple of feet or so above the hook, and, when cast, the line drawn in by hand until the resistance of the shot is felt. The line is then held in the fingers until a bite is felt.

fixed-spool reel – a reel of modern design in which the spool does not rotate to retrieve the line. The line is wound onto the spool by a wire 'bale arm', while in many, the spool moves in and out on a cam, to ensure even distribution of the line, with less chance of tangling.

Reels of similar design are used for both freshwater and sea-fishing, the difference being that the sea-fishing reels are larger, with the drum large enough to take lots of heavy-weight line.

flake – a piece of bread used as a bait, squeezed together to make it stay on the hook, but otherwise unadulterated.

flight – a tackle, usually multi-hooked, used for dead-baiting, which makes the bait move naturally.

> **float** – a device used to hold a baited line so that the bait is dangled at the required depth in the water, and to give an indication when the bait has been taken by a fish.
>
> The float is usually flexibly fixed to the line so that its position can be varied at will, in order that different depths can be fished. Floats are made of a variety of materials, from natural quills, feather stems, wood, cork, and plastics.

floatant *(also 'flotant')* – commercially available (or, occasionally, home-made) preparation applied to an artificial fly or the cast in order to make it float.

float creep – the tendency for the float, particularly top-and-bottom fixed floats secured with rubber bands, to slide down the line towards the hook with the movements involved in striking and casting. This can be obviated by pinching on a small shot beneath the float - this has the added benefit of making the float cock up quickly.

float fishing – fishing by means of dangling a baited hook at the required depth by suspending it beneath a float, as opposed to legering, which dispenses with the float.

Obviously, by its very nature, legering means fishing on the bottom, but float fishing allows the angler to present his bait at any depth.

float legering – a combination of float fishing and legering, in which a float is used, but allowed to run free on the line, without being fixed, or at the most limited in its upward travel along the line by the use of a stop-knot. A useful method of fishing wide, slow-moving rivers, or deep ponds and reservoirs, suitable for use with a paternoster or a straight-through leger rig.

floating bait – any bait that will float naturally can be fished either using a freeline, or anchored to the bottom with a small weight or shot fixed slightly higher up the line than the water's depth, in order to give the bait a little freedom to float where it will.

floating diver – a diver with a lightweight, usually wooden body, and a medium sized vane at the nose to make it dive.

The lure lies on the surface until retrieved, when it dives, the steepness and depth of the dive being influenced by the speed of retrieval.

floating line – a fly line that floats on the water. There are two main types – those that sit on top of the water, and those that float in the surface film. The latter are preferable, as they cast less of a shadow below the water.

Floating lines are used to present a fly that requires no more movement than slowly sinking, or being quickly retrieved, so that it skips over the surface.

floating plug – a light lure, usually of wood, fished near to the bank, to imitate a distressed fish.

CULINARY GUIDANCE

Boiled fish

Place fish in pan and add just enough water to cover the fish. Add a little salt.

Two or three peppercorns and a bay leaf will add flavour. Bring the water to the boil, then simmer – allow about 10-20 minutes per kilo depending on the thickness of the fish. Serve with a garnish of parsley and a sauce of your choice.

floods – in streams over rocky or gravelly ground, floods have very little effect except to make the water deeper, and perhaps faster-moving. A river flowing though clay or loam country, however, will pick up sediments and silts that, in flood, make the water very cloudy.

It is only at the peak period of a flood that fishing is difficult, for when the flood is abating, and the solid particles are falling to the bottom (fining), there will be plenty of food (worms, insects, etc.). The fish will start to feed again, having used lots of energy in fighting the currents.

flounder – *pleuronectes flesus,* also known as the fluke, or butt. A flatfish, it spends the first few weeks of its life looking quite ordinarily fish-like, with a torpedo shaped body, and an eye either side of its head.

The left eye starts to move around to join the other eye, and the body flattens, and the fish takes up residence on the sea-bed.

The colouration varies according to area and habitat, but it is mostly brown or blackish-brown, with a white underside. Usually making a good size – average 1.5 to 2kg (3 to 5lb), the flounder is an inshore fish, favouring the brackish to fresh water of estuaries, and can even be found a surprising distance up-river.

An unsporting method of catching flounder is to wade in the shallows on a falling tide, and just pick them up – something a keen angler would never do! However, this is an indication that they can easily be seen and targeted.

A wide range of baits will take flounder, from crab to limpets, sandeel to ragworm, and, as the fish is a waiter (it lies around on the bottom waiting for its food to drift by, rather than going out to hunt it), the bait should be fished this way, without too heavy a weight, or try a baited spoon. Do not be in a hurry to strike, as flounder are very cautious, and will mouth the bait before taking it.

Occasionally confused with the dab, it can be differentiated by the shallow curve of the lateral line over the pectoral fin, and the feel of the skin which is smooth when the fingertips are run from tail to head, in the dab this being rough.

Like the dab, though, they make good eating.

flowing trace – a long (1 to 1.5 metre/3 to 4ft) length of line of lower breaking strain than the rest of the line, to which the hook is attached, used below the weight and any swivels on straight-through legers.

fly – any flying insect, except for the flying ant, many of which find their way over water, falling prey to several species of fish. It is to emulate these that artificial flies are made, in the process known as fly-dressing, to try to fool fish into taking a disguised hook.

fly-dressing – although trout- and salmon-flies are commercially available, many game fishermen like to tie their own, a process known as fly-dressing. The number and variety of flies, and the techniques involved, make it a subject for many specialised books.

fly-line – a heavyweight line, usually tapered for the last 3-3.6m (10-12ft) towards the tip, with the last foot or so level, the taper allowing the line to be laid lightly on the water at the end of the cast. The line is made heavy to facilitate casting, as the fly weighs next to nothing, and a very light cast is used. The use of a heavy line gives similar control to that of using a stock-whip, although it is best to avoid lashing the water!

Fly-lines used to be made of horsehair, later with a horsehair/silk mix, then silk. Cotton was also used, as was a cotton/silk mix, and all these materials demanded considerable maintenance – they had to be wound onto drying frames after use, and treated with linseed oil, the silk lines having to be polished with the oil.

The trace or cast, the short part between the line and the fly, was made of 'catgut', which had to be soaked in water overnight to make it flexible enough for use. Modern lines are plaited or braided in Terylene or Dacron, and waterproofed with a coating of PVC (polyvinyl chloride).

The plasticizer in this material leaches out with time and use, but it can be replaced with a special lubricant. As these lines float naturally, sinking lines are produced by adding powdered metal to the PVC.

Fly-lines are sold according to grade, to a code agreed by the A.F.T.M., the Association of Fishing Tackle Manufacturers, the code numbers denoting the actual physical weights of the line, with letter suffixes denoting the properties of the line (floating, sinking), and a letter prefix showing the type (taper, etc.).

See table:

Number	Weight in grains	Tolerance in grains	Prefixes
1	60	54 - 66	L - level line(parallel)
2	80	74 - 86	DT - double taper
3	100	94 - 106	WF - weight forward
4	120	114 - 126	ST - shooting taper
			(shooting head)
5	140	132 - 146	
6	160	152 - 168	Suffixes
7	185	177 - 193	
8	210	202 - 218	F - floating
9	240	230 - 250	S - sinking
10	280	270 - 290	I - intermediate
			(needs greasing to float)
11	330	318 - 342	
12	380	368 - 392	F/S - fast sinking
			VFS - very fast sinking

Thus: WF-7-F means weight forward, no. 7, floating
DT-5-S means double taper, no. 5, sinking

These weights are for the length of line usually sold, 27.4 metres (90 feet)

Level Line is a parallel line with no taper – not much used nowadays, their only virtue being inexpensiveness. They can be useful for wet-fly fishing with a following wind.

Double Taper Lines have a taper at both ends, so that the line can be reversed when it wears out.

Weight Forward, also known as 'forward taper lines', have most of their weight at the forward end of the line, the first 9m (30ft) or so being similar to the end of a Double Taper line, fining down to a lighter fly-line for the last 12m (40ft) This is used when casting into the wind. Of late, lines with more than 9m (30ft) of heavy line at the front – are being called 'long belly lines".

Shooting Head or Shooting Taper are made up from half a Double Taper line attached to a length of 9-14kg (20-30lb) breaking strain nylon monofilament with a needle knot that is smoothed over with a whipping varnish. Thus two lines can be made from one Double Taper, giving a similar performance to a Weight Forward line. Used for making long casts in reservoir fishing.

---

fly reel – most reels used in fly-fishing are simple, centre pin reels, with a ratchet or check inbuilt, with the drum caged or enclosed.

fly-tying vice – small device that clamps to a table, with tiny pointed jaws, used to hold the hook around which a fly is tied in the process of fly-dressing.

> **fog** – water vapour at ground- or sea-level. A danger to sailors or fishermen in small boats, with the possibilities of getting lost, or run down by a larger vessel.
>
> Fog can also present problems to the angler fishing off shallow beaches, as in such areas there can be some distance between high and low tides, and the tide can rise at an alarming rate, leaving slightly raised banks of sand isolated, while filling depressions further up the beach, thus cutting the angler off.

forward-swing cast – method of casting for use where no great distance is required, or where overhead foliage impedes a normal overhead cast.

The rod is held upright, open the balearm, let line out to about the length of the rod.

Holding the line at the reel, move the rod backwards slightly, then forward, with a slight dip of the rod hand, letting go of the line. Close the balearm as soon as the cast is completed.

foul-hooking – accidentally hooking a fish in any part of its body other than the mouth – mostly done by striking too quickly when a shoal of fish merely brushes by the line without taking the bait.

> **free fishing** – the only free fishing available in the British Isles is to be found around the coasts – sea-fishing costs nothing yet, unless you are using a private beach, or a privately owned pier or harbour wall.

Fishing in any inland water demands the purchase of at least a rod licence, available from the National River Authority through tackle shops, Post Offices, and Tourist Information Offices.

There are a few locations where ancient rights allow fishing on particular stretches of water, but these are few and far between, and some charge is usually made locally wherever you go, sometimes through the local tackle shop, or even the newsagent's.

Membership of a fishing club will put you right on local charges, and will probably save you money, as they often own the rights, and reduce fees for members.

freelining – fishing with nothing on the line but the baited hook – the bait needs to be big enough to allow the line to be tightened against its drag, to allow transmission of the vibrations that will indicate a bite. Freelining can also be used with a floating bait.

French boom – a paternoster boom made of wire bent to a triangular shape with a loop at each end of the base and an inward loop in the middle, around which the line is wound, with a further loop wound at the apex of the triangle, to which the cast or hook-length is attached.

Popular because it is easily and quickly attached, and can be placed anywhere on the line, allowing the angler to vary easily and quickly the depths at which he fishes.

fresh water – water in any lake, pond, river or stream not affected by sea-water – in river estuaries, the only freshwater fish that will be found are salmon, sea-trout, and silver eels (the sea-going, mature freshwater eel).

freshwater mussels – bi-valves, shellfish with two shells, the half-dozen or so species of freshwater mussel found in the British Isles all make good baits. Open the mussel live with a knife and cut out the flesh, or boil lightly for a few minutes.

The largest mussel found here is the swan mussel, *anodonta cygnea,* which can grow to 15 cm (6in) across, with a brown shell more reminiscent of the more familiar bi-valves, hinged in the middle.

The others are all more or less the normal mussel-shape, hinged near the end, including the pearl mussel – check this one for your fortune before using for bait!

Tench, barbel, carp, roach, and rudd all fall to mussel bait. It is not generally appreciated that, before attaching itself to a rock on the bottom, the mussel has a free-swimming phase in which it attaches itself parasitically to larger fish. Thus, if there are mussels around, there will be fish!

freshwater shrimp – *gammarus pulex,* excellent bait for roach, bream, and dace. These tiny shrimps are found in weed, particularly silkweed, where they are sought out avidly by fish and their fry.

Difficult to get on the hook, but worthwhile. If a clump of weed can be pulled up, shake it out over a sheet of plastic, to dislodge the shrimp. With the freshwater shrimp as part of their diet, the flesh of the trout takes on a pink hue.

freshwater weeds – part of their habitat, the fish use weeds as cover, shelter, a larder, and itself as food. The only nuisance value in weed occurs when your tackle is tangled in it, or loose weed in flood conditions hangs around your line – so don't leger in dense weedbanks.

fur – hairs from the pelts of various mammals are used in amateur fly-dressing, among the most common being rabbit, mole, and squirrel.

gaff – large hook on a handle used to land large fish, particularly where circumstances preclude the use of a landing net, such as a boat with a high freeboard, or a harbour wall, or a groyne. Out of fashion nowadays as being cruel, it also damages what might be a specimen fish, but is useful where the large fish has large, sharp teeth and an aggressive disposition.

gag – device made from spring-steel wire, having two parallel arms with a loop wound in the middle, so that it is inclined to spring apart unless held by a sliding keeper.

The gag is used to keep the jaws of a fish open while a deeply taken or swallowed hook is removed, particularly in the case of large fish with dangerous teeth, such as a pike.

Commercially available gags do have one major drawback, in that the outward-bent jaws of the gag are for some reason finished with sharp prongs, which must do damage to, and hurt, the fish. Blunt or tape them over.

gammarus pulex – the common freshwater shrimp is notable for two reasons. Firstly, many fish eat them, so they make good bait, and secondly, along with the water snail, their presence in the diet of the trout gives the flesh of the trout a pink tinge.

game fishing – angling for any of the fish deemed 'game', i.e., salmon, trout, sea-trout. The grayling, a salmonid, is sometimes rated as a game fish, sometimes included among the coarse fish.

garfish – *belone belone,* a long, slender, silvery-green, eel-like fish with an elongated toothed beak of a mouth, the garfish is not very big, but a fish of about 450g (1lb) will measure around 50cm (20in).

Garfish move north into British waters in the spring, where they spawn in the shallows, and provide good sport for anglers on piers, rocks, or boats. Most fun can be had using light spinning tackle, or drift-lining, and an interesting variation of float-fishing, in which a weighted line is cast, then a short line carrying a baited hook and a float is clipped on and allowed to slide down the main to the surface.

Like mackerel, these fish will go for anything silvery and moving, or any of the usual sea-fishing baits, particularly herring or a lask of mackerel, sandeel, or prawn.

> Garfish are good to eat, if you can ignore the other peculiarity of this odd-looking fish – it has green bones, which some people find off-putting.

gentles – Euphemism for maggots.

German sprat – an artificial lure, a type of spoon, used primarily in fishing for pollack.

gillaroo – a variation of the common trout, found in Ireland.

gilt-head – *sparus aurata,* a member of the bream family, it only visits British waters occasionally and is easily identified by the strip of gold scales between the eyes. Not very big, 0.5kg (1lb).

golden carp – a decorative version of the common carp, this albino form of the fish is also called the hi-goi. Under good conditions the golden carp can reach considerable proportions, with a deeper body than the wild common form.

golden orfe – *leusicus idus,* a member of the cyprinid family, this is a reddish coloured version of the silver orfe. Not native to Britain, any of these found will be introductions or escapees from private ponds.

It prefers clean waters, and is much sought after by anglers in its native regions, central Europe, reaching as far north as Siberia and Finland. In some parts, especially in the lower reaches of the larger rivers, it is fished commercially.

goldfish – *carassius auratus,* a member of the cyprinid family, closely related to the crucian carp Escapees from captivity are occasionally found, and can grow to quite a size in the wild.

goldsinny – *ctenolabrus rupestris,* a small wrasse, up to 15cm (6in) long, similar to the corkwing, but of a drab yellowish colour, with a small dark spot just in front of the caudal fin, above the lateral line. Common only in the west and south west of the British Isles.

golden tench – a bright yellow variety of the common tench. Not at all common, there is an example (stuffed) at Overbeck House, near Salcombe, Devon, a National Trust museum.

goose-quill floats – if obtainable, the goose quill (the spine of the pinion feathers from a goose's wing), furnished with a balsawood body, makes an excellent, delicate float, suitable for slow-moving or still waters.

gozzers – one of the 'special' maggots, bred and fed on pigeon breasts or similar for preference, producing a fat, soft, white grub, particularly effective as a bream bait.

grasshopper – used live, an extremely good bait for game fish at periods of low water, on a very fine hook. The grasshopper should be used as a dry-fly would be used, on a floating line, fished up-stream on slow-moving or still water.

---

gravel pits – these are the derelict workings left when the gravel supplies extracted from them are exhausted, or beyond economical working. The empty holes are then filled with water as an amenity, usually by agreement with the local authority, as part of the planning permission granted for the workings.

Gravel pit fishing is like no other, in that by their very nature, they do not follow the natural contours of the surrounding land, so to start with, underwater contours are hard to predict.

The types of fish vary from one pit to another, and it may take many visits, and much experimentation, to probe the depths and possibilities of any particular pit.

grayling – *thymallus thymallus,* a member of the salmonid family, having the tiny adipose fin behind a large, sail-like dorsal fin, the grayling is sometimes treated as a game fish, at others as a coarse fish.

It is encouraged in some areas in what would be considered game waters, while in others it is considered a nuisance as it competes for the food of its cousin, the trout.

An elegant fish with silvery blue/green scales with occasional black spots, easily distinguished by its large, sail-like dorsal fin, the grayling is a gregarious fish and moves about in shoals, preferring clean, strong-flowing water.

It is best angled for on trotting tackle, and will also take wet- or dry-flies and nymphs. A strong fighter, it has soft lips, and its maxilliary bones are less stout than those of the trout, so care must be taken not to rip out the hook.

> Good eating, the flavour of its flesh is reflected in its Latin name.

greased-line fishing – so-called because the line had to be greased in order to make it float – not necessary nowadays with modern floating lines – this is a fly-fishing method most suited to 'low-water' summer conditions, with bright sunlight, still water, and good visibility for the fish. The line floats, and is fished with a sinking tackle and a small fly.

Greenland shark – *somniosus microcephalus,* a shark that prefers cold water, there is no record of a rod-and-line capture of this shark in British waters.

grey mullet – *mugil cephalus,* the common grey mullet is only one of four grey mullet species found in British waters, and is distinguished by having transparent eyelids.

The thin-lipped grey mullet, *mugil capito,* is a small species which has a patch of yellow scales on its head extending as far as the upper lip, and thin lips, which distinguish it from the thick-lipped grey mullet, *chelon labrosus,* which has a thick, puffy upper lip.

The golden grey mullet *liza auratus,* has a similar golden patch to that of the thin-lipped, but it does not extend to the upper lip. All the grey mullet are cautious, shy fish, found around harbours, inlets, and estuaries, and should be fished for on light tackle. Freshwater tackle is often sufficient, using worms, breadpaste or flakes, and, where the fish come into harbour looking for the grubs of the flies that breed on the seaweed that dries out at low tide, maggots have been found effective.

When hooked they can be powerful fighters, but care must be taken, as they have soft lips, and the hook can tear out easily. Opinions vary as to their palatability, with some decrying them, while others claim that grey mullet make good eating, but take on flavours.

grilse – a young, maiden salmon that is returning to the river after a spell at sea - this can be between one and four years. The colouration will be silver all over, overlaid with a purple sheen, and its tail will still have a slight cleft. As young salmon increase in size rapidly at sea (a smolt leaving the river at a few ounces will, within a year, increase its weight fifteen-fold, and after two years can reach 3.6-4.5kg (8 to 10lbs), while a three year grilse will be about 6.8-8.1kg (15-18lb). The grilse does not become a salmon until it has spawned for the first time.

groin protector – also known as a butt pad, a contrivance similar to that used to carry a flag in parades, a socket on a padded leather patch, fixed to a belt, and worn to carry the butt of the rod when big-game fishing, giving the angler a fulcrum against which to lever.

grip leads – flat, circular weights with short spiky protuberances, used when sea-fishing over muddy bottoms.

Of no use for casting great distances, they give a good grip when lowered from a boat or pier, and are not prone to being rolled around by currents. Invariably the type of weight supplied with crab lines. Also known as watch leads.

ground – in sea-anglers' parlance, the sea-bottom.

ground fishing – fishing with your bait on the bottom.

ground-bait – a bread or meal based mixture either purchased from a shop, or home-made, designed to break up in the water having been thrown in as a wet ball or bolus, offering the promise of food without giving enough substance to satisfy the fish, but encouraging them into the area in the hope of food.

Larger pieces of bait can be incorporated if desired, such as maggots, if these are being used on the hook. A catapult can be used to take the groundbait further than can be reached with hand-thrown bait.

gudgeon – *gobio gobio*, a member of the cyprinid family, the gudgeon is a small, not very pretty, fish, with two barbels at the ends of its upper lip, and is often mistaken for a young barbel, but with its cylindrical body, and only two, as opposed to the four barbs of the barbel, identification should not be difficult.

Colouration varies, but is generally silvery with grey or brown speckles, with darker splotches along the flanks, above the lateral line. Not usually angled for, except by small boys along canal banks, the gudgeon can be a useful bait-fish, being easily caught.

It has a certain nuisance value, as it will nibble at large baits intended for bigger fish. The largest caught in England is 140g (5oz), so the coarse angler looking to get his name in the record books stands every chance – these fish grow to about 300g (10-11ozs) in Continental waters.

gurnard – there are three types, or colours, of gurnard, the grey *eutrigla gurnardus*, the red *aspitrigla cuculus*, and the yellow or Tub, *trigla lucerna*.

Bizarre, striking fish, they must be quite old in geological terms, as they retain the wedge-shaped, bonily armour-plated fore-ends seen in fossil fish. Part of their pectoral fins has mutated into finger-like feelers that investigate the bottom as they hunt for the small crustacea, molluscs and worms that make up their diet.

All the commonly used sea baits will catch them, and the grey and red provide a good meal, but the flesh is too fine-textured to stand boiling or poaching – try baking them.

The grey gurnard is the smallest, growing to about 0.5kg (1lb), the red attaining 1 to 2kg (2 to 4lb) and the yellow gets quite big, 0.5-5kg+ (11+lb).

The yellow, the handsomest, with its yellow-gold overall colouring and blue pectoral fins, is not usually eaten.

hackle – the part of an artificial fly made from a feather to resemble the legs and feelers of a real fly. The feather is prepared for hackling by running the fingers along the fibres, separating them and turning them so that they do not join back together.

haddock – *melanogrammus aeglefinus,* a member of the cod family, the haddock is distinguishable by the black spot on the lateral line just above the pectoral fin and the tall, pointed primary dorsal fin. A silvery grey all over, the haddock is found all round the British Isles, especially in northern waters.

Growing up to 4kg (8.8lb), it feeds on small fish and crustacea preferring rough, rocky ground. Small fish, crabs, marine worms, and shellfish, are good baits, and the fish are also caught on pirks or jigs.

> Haddock are good to eat, and an important fish commercially, being a favourite in the fried fish trade. Smoked, it is a popular delicacy, but if you try home-smoking, do not expect to arrive at that bright yellow – it is colouring.

hair rig – a very delicate method of fishing in which the bait is tied under the hook with a fine piece of line. Used for fish that test the bait by mouthing it before biting, it also has the advantage of not masking the point of the hook.

hake – *merluccius merluccius,* a member of the cod family, found all round the British Isles except for the upper English Channel, this silvery fish, which eats a variety of smaller fish, is rarely caught by anglers, but is a useful commercial fish, in some parts of Britain taking precedence in popularity over cod and haddock.

Caught – when it is caught – on rod and line, on pirks and jigs, or on small fish baits.

halibut – *hippoglossus hippoglossus,* the largest of the flatfish, usually included among the game fish.

Growing up to 2.30 metres (7ft 6in) and weights of over 130kg (300lb), the halibut is a fish that prefers deep Arctic waters, so the intrepid halibut fisherman will need to travel to Scottish and Northern Irish waters, although the west coast of Ireland and Cornwall could prove fruitful.

It feeds on other flatfish, large shellfish, haddock, pollack, whiting, wrasse and codling, and all of these make good bait, used either live or dead. If used dead, they must be made to appear life-like.

Really heavy tackle will be needed, and the rod will need to be fitted with a steel-roller tip ring. A heavy duty multiplier reel is essential, carrying at least 80lb BS terylene line. As the halibut prefers a moving bait, the usual method adopted is drift fishing, with the bait close to the bottom.

> The halibut is a superb culinary fish, but the flesh can be a little dry for some tastes. Try it with a light lemon and cream sauce, or poached in white wine, finishing the sauce with cream and egg yolks.

hammerhead shark – *sphyrna zygaena,* one of the larger sharks found in British waters, growing up to 400+kg (880+lb), there is only an unsubstantiated claim to a rod and line catch of this unmistakable fish, which has its eyes on the extremities of its flattened, sideways elongated head.

hand-lining – fishing without the use of a rod. In instances where a rod is unavailable, or would be an encumbrance, such as in a cramped boat with a lot of rigging, hand-lining comes into its own.

Retrieval of line can be quicker than with a reel, and when heavy leads that might throw too much strain on a rod, it is the only way of fishing. *See also crab-lines.*

handling fish – the scales and mucus on the skin of a fish are there for a purpose, and care should be taken with any fish that it is intended should be returned to the water.

Handle with a soft, damp cloth where possible, or wet hands if necessary, and place rather than throw the fish into the keep net. When emptying the keep net, simply lower the top ring below water level, preferably facing upstream, allowing the fish to swim away.

If the fish are required for weighing or photography, they should be lifted out individually rather than being tipped out.

hand-tailing – when landing large fish, particularly salmon, in certain circumstances it is possible to land the fish without the use of the gaff or landing net. If the water is shallow enough and the bank configuration such that the fish can be reached, hand-tailing, properly carried out, will land the fish safely.

The fish is grasped around the caudle peduncle, the 'wrist' just in front of the tail, preferably with the thumb/forefinger loop facing towards the tail, as this is the stronger position, allowing an easier lift.

Be sure of your foot-hold, and beware of slipped discs. Oddly, this practice does not work with the sea-trout, as the contour of the 'wrist' is unsuitable.

harbours – many types of fish are attracted to harbours as habitats by reason of the sheltered waters, the large stocks of small marine life and human detritus that provide food (particularly in places that do not dry out completely).

Harbour walls provide good anchorage for limpets, barnacles, mussels, and the weed that holds myriads of small marine animals. They also contain nooks and crannies in which fish hide, ranging from tiny rock gobies to enormous conger eels.

Harbours are also favourite haunts of grey mullet, bass, pollack, and even cod. The harbour wall, by its very nature a place where the water is deep, precludes the necessity for long casts – fish tend to hang around the wall in search of food – so they are excellent places for young anglers to learn the sport and the handling of their rods and tackle; relatively safe, reasonably sheltered, and convenient for the bait and tackle shop should things go wrong.

In most instances there is no fee for fishing from harbour walls.

A centre-pin or multiplier reel on a short pier rod or boat rod will suffice, and the ubiquitous crab line has introduced many a young angler to the sport on a harbour wall.

The paternoster rig is a favourite method of fishing in these circumstances, or in really sheltered harbours a light float tackle.

There are a few drawbacks to harbour fishing. Harbours are busy places – they are, after all, built for the convenience of boats and boatmen, not anglers – so be prepared to be disturbed.

harbours – *continued*

Harbour walls are usually tall affairs, depending on the local range of the tide, so it could happen on occasion that a sizeable fish has to be hauled up a considerable height – a gaff, although brutal, would be invaluable here.

> Finally, many harbours lack any safety railing, and can be very slippery, so watch your (and the little one's) footing.

haywire twist – wire fishing lines cannot be tied like more flexible nylon lines, by reason of their rigidity, and the fact that such knots would weaken the line. The haywire twist will hold such lines fast without weakening them.

The working end of the wire line is passed through the link that will take the trace, then passed again, to make a double turn. It is then wound around its standing part at least ten times, the end being coiled about to finish off, then cut flush.

hearing – the hearing apparatus of the fish is quite sophisticated, and is connected directly to the skin of the animal, requiring no external ears.

In some fish the swim bladder, inflated like a balloon, transmits pressure change information to the brain, as do the mucus-filled sacs of the lateral line. In this way, the whole fish is a hearing mechanism.

Semi-circular canals within the hearing are used to convey balance and acceleration information to the brain. Small wonder, then, that the seasoned angler looks askance at those inconsiderate enough to take a portable radio fishing, or little boys who lob rocks into the swim.

hempseed – the seed of the hemp plant, which, though it does not contain any of the narcotic substances or properties of its mother plant, seems to be addictive to some fish.

They are boiled until they split and the inside is soft, and is then pushed on to the hook until the point emerges from the other side. One drawback of using hempseed is that some fish appear to mistake the shot used to weight the line for the bait, giving false bites.

One way round this problem is to use lead wire wrapped round the line, or the 'mouse-droppings' type of weight.

herling – one of the many local names for the young sea-trout returning to the river after a season at sea. *See also finnock, sewin, whitling, sprod, and peal.*

herring – *clupea harengus,* this small fish, which grows up to 1kg (2.2lb), is seldom caught by the angler, but is of interest here as it is useful as bait, either whole or in strip or lask form.

Of great commercial value, it has been in decline in recent years, owing to over-fishing, but is now making a recovery.

Hi-D line – a fast-sinking fly-line, designed to sink at about 30cm (1ft) to 3 seconds.

Hi-goi – an albino version of the common carp, *cyprinus carpio,* to which it is similar in most respects except colour, these were selectively bred for decorative purposes.

hitches – a hitch is a knot or method of tying a rope, string or line to a spar, stick or rod.

hold-alls – when buying a tackle-bag, it pays to buy as capacious a bag as you can afford, as fishing tackle has a habit of multiplying without human assistance.

It should have some method of separating individual items (boxes, pockets, etc), ensuring that no tangles arise – there is nothing worse than trying to sort out that particular piece of equipment, while another angler is hooking 'em out by the dozen a few yards along the bank.

Washability is important, as these bags can get rather mucky, and comfort of carrying is a strong factor, as the best fishing spot is invariably a long walk from the nearest parking place. Lastly, built-in sit-on-ability is an added bonus.

hollow glass rods – after decades in which bamboo or cane ruled as the material of preference for fishing rods, in the 1960s glass re-inforced plastics (GRP) became available.

The first rods of this modern fabric were of solid construction, and these rods were robust and fairly maintenance-free, but lacked the responsiveness of the old cane or split-cane rods. These solid rods gave way to rods of hollow construction, which now hold sway.

As they are made by being wound on a mandrel, and smoothed to give a presentable finish, it is possible to add or subtract glass cloth and/or resin at different parts of the rod in order to affect its action.

hooks – the business end of any angler's tackle, the part that meets the fish. Considering the importance of this close juxtaposition, little time and attention is paid to, and little money is spent on this item. More care taken in the selection of hooks, and less scrimping and saving on what is already the cheapest part of the tackle may turn those "one-that-got-away" stories into landed fish.

The scale on which hooks are sized is not completely standardised, but generally speaking freshwater hooks are made in sizes annotated by the Redditch Scale (also known as the Old Scale), using the even numbers down from 24 to 2, the smaller numbers representing progressively larger hooks – a size 20, for instance, being about 3mm (.125in) long, a no. 12 is 1cm (.375in), and a 2 is about 2cm (.75in).

The larger sizes are then numbered from 1/0 upwards – 2/0, 3/0, and so on up to size 12/0.

A New Scale was introduced a few years ago, and caused confusion as the numbers differed, and anglers did not always specify to which scale they were referring.

Hooks fall into three distinct types; eyed hooks, spade-ended hooks, and ready-tied hooks. Within these categories there are several different shapes; the curve of the bend, the type of point/barb combination, the set of the eye or spade, all differing in what were originally local variations, or adaptations thought up by fly-dressers.

The parts of the hook are as follows: below the eye, or spade, comes the shank, the straight part that curves into the bend, which travels up past the barb to the point. The space between the point and the shank is called the gap or gape, and the depth from the inside of the bend to the level of the point is called the throat.

hooks – *continued*

The eye of a hook can be set straight, that is in the same level as the shank; or 'upturned' (also called 'turned out'), which means it is bent outwards from the body of the hook; or down-turned (also 'turned in'), or bent inwards to the body of the hook.

The reason for these differences involves the way the hook sits on the line, and the uses to which the hook is put – for instance, a fly tied on a hook with an upturned eye will land more lightly on the water, while the line loops off the surface, giving no tell-tale line near it; a wet-fly on a down-turned hook will appear more natural underwater.

Eyed hooks are best tied on the line with the half-blood knot or a hook snood, and care must be taken to use a hook with the right size of eye, one which closely takes the thickness of line being used.

Spade ended hooks have to be whipped on to the line with a spade-whipping, which is fiddly, and best done before your expedition.

Ready-tied hooks come with their own cast or trace, factory tied, and should be inspected to make sure that the whipping butts right up to the shoulder, which holds it steady – whipping that stops short can allow the hook to rotate, and could lose that fish!

Hook types have evolved for different uses, according sometimes to whim – the crystal has a bend that curves normally then angles sharply, and is said to penetrate easily, but the sharp bend renders it weaker than a round bend, which is preferred by many anglers as it gives plenty of room for several worms or maggots.

The Model Perfect has an offset point which is reputed to give better 'hold'.

These offsets are known as 'kirbed' (offset to the left when viewed from the top, 'reversed' when bent to the right, and 'straight' when not offset at all.)

Points and barbs vary, as does the distance between them. The hollow point has a concave curve between point and barb, the Dublin has a point that curves slightly back from the barb, the knife edge is straight and sharpened like a knife, the curve is bent in towards the shank, and the superior is straight from barb to point.

The distance between point and barb is critical – too great, and the hook acts as if barbless, too small and the angle between the two makes penetration difficult. Look out too for barbs that are cut too deeply – this can weaken the hook.

The length of the shank and the thickness of the wire used to make the hook are important insofar as the hook's ability to carry bait is concerned.

Some baits need long shanks – casters, lobworms, breadpaste, etc, while maggots need a short shank. Casters also require a fine wire hook, as thicker hooks will ruin this delicate bait.

Remember also that the length of shank affects penetration owing to the angle between eye (or spade) and the point – a short shanked hook penetrates more deeply, while needing greater initial effort in the strike, while a long shank will give quicker but shallower penetration.

Discard any corroded or rusted hooks, and keep those in your box sharp – a small carborundum stone is inexpensive – and store them stuck in a cork.

> Hooks left lying around in the tackle box get themselves and other items into a tangle, and can lead to injury in the sorting out. By the same token, resist any advice that tells you to test a hook's temper and sharpness against your thumbnail – it is not a very consistent measure of temper, and you could find out about the sharpness the hard way!

hook lengths – not the length of the hook, but a short lighter piece of line between the hook and the main line. Also known as a trace.

houting – *coregonus lavaretus oxyrhyncus,* a marine member of the whitefish family, rare in British waters, but well known in the coastal regions of Northern France, the Low Countries, and Scandinavia. These torpedo-shaped, herring-like fish, which still ascend rivers to spawn, are greyish/blue or green, fading to a silvery yellow on the flanks and belly.

The head is small, with a pronounced blue/black snout, the mouth being pushed back. Apparently tasty, this fish is too rare in British waters to eat.

huchen – *hucho hucho,* a member of the salmonidae family, unknown in British waters, the huchen is a non-migratory inhabitant of the rivers of central Europe.

It is more closely related to the char end of the salmon-trout family salvelinus, although it resembles the sea-trout, growing, however, to far greater sizes, up to 18kg (40lb) in restricted waters, 45kg (100lb) in such waters as the Danube.

Owing to these large sizes, and the fighting characteristics inherent in the salmon family, this fish is much sought after by intrepid anglers, being caught usually on live-bait, or by trolling.

hybrids – many fish, particularly those of the same families, interbreed, usually accidentally. In the carp family cyprinidae, this can lead to confusion as to just which one has been caught.

Bream, roach, rudd, dace, chub, and bleak can all be found shoaling together, or in specie shoals in close proximity, and at spawning time they can mingle at the edges of the shoals, the males of one species fertilizing the eggs of another.

The resulting hybrids carry characteristics of both parents in varying degrees, which has in the past resulted in mistaken claims for record or specimen fish. Differentiation between most of these hybrids depends on fin-ray counting, as colouration can be misleading.

icthyologist – a person who practises icthyology. It is to these scientists that we owe most of our knowledge of the habits of fish – for instance, before two Italian icthyologists called Calandruccio and Grazzi studied the movements and breeding habits of the common European eel during the latter years of the 19th century, the life cycle of this animal was a total mystery.

icthyology – the science or study of fishes.

injecting baits – the practice of making a bait fish more olfactorily attractive (smelling better!) by injecting it with a pungent fish oil, such as pilchard.

injuries – the injuries that arise from fishing are primarily: laceration (hooks in various parts of the anatomy, cuts from knives, bites from large, toothy fish, etc); immersion (falling in, drowning); contusion (being hit in the face by half a pound of lead weight by a clumsy caster is no joke); and their peripherals – septiceamia (blood poisoning) following laceration, hypothermia as a result of being wet in cold conditions after immersion.

> First aid is useful training in all walks of life, and some knowledge of how to treat simple injuries is of great value in any pursuit in which the participant is alone or in inaccessible places, as is often the case in angling.
>
> Furthermore, time and place of injury are important – a simple injury on a riverbank assumes major proportions when it occurs ten miles offshore in adverse weather conditions – and bear in mind that to the usual angler's injuries can be added a whole new list as soon as you start doing it in boats.

insurance – in spite of the dire warnings given above in respect of injuries, insurance against the angler clouting someone with a weighted line, or hooking a spectator, is usually quite inexpensive. Just as important, perhaps, is insurance for your tackle, some of which can be quite expensive (depending upon how deeply you get into the sport), against accidental damage, loss, or theft.

introduced fish – fish that are not native to a country. It is sometimes problematical to decide which fish are introduced, and which have arrived by the often bizarre machinations of nature, but there are some very obvious introductions, particularly decorative fish.

However, there have been introductions for commercial reasons – the carp was brought to the British Isles during the middle ages, probably by monasteries, by reason of its palatability, speed of growth, and general good response to lack of husbandry. Later introductions of this fish were made with the angler specifically in mind.

Jardines – a spiral lead or non-toxic weight cast around a brass or copper wire which is also spiralled at each end. The line is wrapped around the weight in its continuous spiral groove.

Used for spinning or dead-baiting where a weight is needed to keep the spinner or bait low in the water, but where low water resistance is required. Jardines come in weights from 25 to 100g (2 to 8 ounces).

Jardines Perfected Snaps – A form of snap-tackle invented by a Mr Horace Hutchinson.

jiggers – a weighted sea-fishing lure, also called a pirk, usually brightly silvered or coloured, fished by jigging it up and down to simulate such as small fish, cuttlefish or squid.

jigging – moving a lure or dead-bait quickly up and down to simulate life – only done, of course, with lures intended to represent animals that move that way in life.

John Dory – *zeus faber,* also known as 'St Peter's Fish' on account of the purplish oval mark on its flank reputed to have been left there by the saint's thumb and forefinger.

A deep-bodied, flattish fish that swims upright rather than on its side, the John Dory is a brilliant golden colour when first caught, fading to the more familiar olive-brown quite quickly.

Unmistakable, with long, trailing rays extending from its dorsal and pectoral fins, the John Dory is common enough around British shores in summer months, but is mostly caught by netting, being uncommonly caught on rod and line, and then usually by accident when fishing for other prey.

> Growing up to 4kg (8.8lb), the John Dory is good to eat, indeed, is considered a delicacy on the Continent.

They will take small fish and shellfish, and to watch the John Dory feed is a revelation – the mouth extrudes, and the prey is sucked in from as much as 18 inches away.

keep net – a large tubular net, kept open in the water by plastic or metal rings at intervals down its length (2 metres or more), made of a knotless mesh so as to avoid damage to the fish that are kept in it for inspection or weighing purposes during a match, or just for counting at the end of the day's fishing.

All such nets must conform to local bye-laws. Fish kept therein should be released by depressing the mouth of the net below water level, not by lifting the fish out.

kelt – a salmon making its way down-river, spent by spawning.

kidney spoon – a spoon lure with the spoon being shaped like the outline of a kidney, an oval with a slight curve to one side. The kidney spoon has a throbbing, pulsating spinning action.

killing fish – most coarse fishermen set out with the intention of returning their catch to the water, either in the mistaken supposition that freshwater fish are not worth eating, or because they are simply there for the sport, and do not wish to kill their quarry.

However, anglers in some arms of the sport refer to certain baits, lures, or flies as being efficient 'killers'; these anglers are usually pike fishermen (by their predatory nature, pike have always been considered pests in some waters, and therefore it was not necessary to return them to the water), game fishermen (salmon and trout are very tasty, and game fishing is expensive, so you deserve to keep what you catch), or sea fishermen (most marine fish are eminently edible).

> The actual process of killing the fish varies with type and size – for most a sharp blow to the head with a blunt instrument, or the application of a sharp knife to the vital organs will suffice, and some fish just give up and die when landed, as they have no mechanism to cope with pressure changes.

However, some fish present problems in this department. Congers, sharks, and, in freshwater, pike, and eels all have sharp teeth, powerful jaws, and muscular bodies.

killing fish – *continued*

If the fish is not too large (the biggest pike you are likely to see will certainly not approach the size of a conger or shark), the use of a gag will save your fingers.

In the case of large marine fish, if size and ferocity are at all off-putting, it is as well to have some suitable container into which the fish can be dropped, and left until nature takes its course – but humane considerations will probably demand that you make as quick an end as possible to the fish, and suffocated fish become flabby, and are reputed not to eat so well. In this case, the receptacle is still advisable, as it restricts the fish's movement.

Most hire-boat skippers will have the means of despatch close to hand.

Kilmore boom – a boom specifically designed for legering, consisting of a wire loop with a swivel to a larger clip-like loop, to which a weight is attached. A hooked trace is attached to the first loop (which can be plain, or ceramic or metal lined). The drawback to this type of boom is that the whole thing is in a straight line, and the trace is so close to the weight that tangles are inevitable.

king carp – a large version of the common carp, *cyprinus carpio,* a secondary introduction during the early part of the 20th century.

The wild carp extant in the British Isles from the middle ages were the result of introduction by monastic orders as a food crop – owing to the lack of transport into the interior of the country, fresh sea fish were not readily available, and carp were favoured because they bred and grew prolifically.

With the advent of faster and more widespread transport, marine fish were distributed more widely, and the necessity of growing fish locally declined, so stew-ponds and their contents were neglected. Not so in Europe, where transport was later in spreading and religious convictions insisting on fish consumption on certain days were stronger.

The carp survived as a commercial proposition, and was selectively bred larger and larger. With the growth of angling as a sport, the size of these fish prompted introductions, and as they are the same species as the original carp, interbreeding has taken place, with myriad results.

Carp can be found from a few kilogrammes in weight up to 20+kg (40 to 50lb).

kingfishers - the Halcyon of Greek legend, this brilliant blue little bird knows a lot more about fishing than any angler.

If it is hunting – sitting on a branch peering down into the stream, and diving – then there are minnows or other small fish shoaling.

Where there are small fish in numbers, there will be the larger fish that feed upon them – your prey!

Kingfisher is also the name of a very successful trout fly.

king rag – a very large (up to and occasionally over 60 cm or 2ft in length) marine worm, with hundreds of 'legs' along the sides. Such is the size that one of these animals can provide several baits, although for such fish as bass or pollack 30cm (1ft) can be used to good effect.

Beware the front end – it contains a retractable pair of nippers that can inflict a painful bite.

Ragworm can be found between high and low water marks, in 'U'-shaped burrows, and will keep for up to a week if cooled, and kept wrapped in newspaper at about 2° C. Preserved specimens are often to be found in bait shops, and if these are used as bait, benefit from an injection of a pungent fish oil.

knot – a method of joining two or more lengths of rope, string, or fishing line. Those of most interest to the angler are the blood knot, the half blood knot (which is really a hitch), the water knot, the loop to loop, the clove hitch, the figure of eight knot, and the needle knot.

Others are also dealt with elsewhere in the text. Also, a knot is a measurement of speed on water - one nautical mile per hour.

> **knotted nets** – nets made of cotton or synthetic fibres that are knotted to form the squares are now illegal in most areas, and with good reason, as the knots act as a very effective abrasive on the mucus and skin of a fish, ripping the poor beasts to shreds.
>
> Discard any such nets, and buy the modern, knotless nets, and do not be tempted to buy the old nets so often seen nowadays at markets.

knotless tapers – the business end of a fly line is the lighter, thinner nylon leader, which steps down in thickness as it gets nearer the fly, in order that the line nearest the fish is thin enough not to frighten it, but strong enough to land it.

This can be done by tying on progressively thinner nylon line, but some anglers prefer the relatively expensive manufactured knotless taper, which obviates the possibility of tangles caused by knots, and generally casts easier.

lamprey – small, eel-like fish, the lampreys are only distantly related to the other fish in the river, lake, or sea. They belong to an ancient order of jawless fish, the Ostracoderms, going back to the Palaeozoic era (the first geological period), having a sucker-like mouth with which they cling onto their victims – other fish, whose blood they suck through incisions made with their primitive teeth.

There are three species of lamprey found in British waters – the sea lamprey, *petromyzon marinus,* the lampern, *lampetra fluviatilis,* and the brook lamprey (also known as Planer's lamprey), *lampetra planeri.* (N.B. the brook lamprey is not parasitic, and appears not to feed during its adult life, using its sucker only to hang onto rocks).

> The lamprey is not a fish of interest to the angler, but was eaten in the middle ages, usually in pies, the whole fish being eaten, as it is boneless.
>
> King Henry I was reputed to have died 'from a surfeit of lampreys' – presumably indigestion, which probably accounts for their decline in favour.

landing net – when fishing with a lightweight line, it is possible to hook, play, and land fish heavier than the declared breaking strain of your line or cast, owing to the fish's buoyancy in water.

However, as the fish is lifted out of the water, the effect of gravity comes fully into play, and the full weight comes to bear on the line. To avoid losing the fish, therefore, a large net on a handle is slid under the fish as is comes towards you, and the fish is lifted out of the water without undue strain being put upon the line.

larvae – the young stage of some aquatic insects, various larvae are an abundant food-source for many fish, and are the basis of several lures and wet-flies.

lask – expression used for a strip of fish taken diagonally from the flank, used for bait. Mackerel or herring are the fish most usually used for this.

lateral line – a line along each flank of the fish, clearly delineated by colouration or scale placement in some fish, unmarked and virtually invisible in others. The lateral line forms part of the fish's sensory equipment, being composed of a series of mucus-filled canals that are used to detect pressure variations and vibrations in the water, acting as an addendum to the hearing system, and can in fact be used to escape from predators, and for finding prey even in experimentally blinded fish.

lay-back or laid-back casting – for extra-long casts when beach-casting, using a multiplier reel. The angler stands at right-angles to the direction he wishes to cast, and the rod is held horizontally at between waist and chest height, pointing inland, with 60cm (2ft) of line out.

Hands should be quite far apart, the right hand stopping the line running out.

The weight is swung gently away from the body, then the rod tip is swung through an arc, the line being released, and the angler's weight being transferred from the right foot to the left, the body swinging to finish facing the direction of the cast.

To avoid the unwanted 'birdsnest' of line at the reel when the bait lands, pressure should be applied to the reel with the right hand, slowing it, when the weight reaches the height of its trajectory, thus avoiding over-run.

laying on – float-fishing, but with the bait and a length of the line and its weights lying on the bottom.

leads – weights under 30g ($1^1/_{16}$ oz) are now made of non-toxic materials, to avoid the poisoning possibilities to animals and birds when swallowed, but all weights are still referred to as leads.

Freshwater and sea-fishing weights differ primarily in size, as the conditions in which they are used differ. Freshwater leads are used as legers, and to weight the line below a float, and as conditions are far less severe than at sea, are much smaller.

The weights used in float-fishing are primarily the split-shot types that are pinched on the line, these corresponding to the shot sizes used in shooting, namely swanshot, AAA, BB, Nos 1,2,3,4,5,6,7,8, (No. 8 is also called 'dust' shot), and a very fine shot called 'micro-dust'.

For those who believe that fish mouth the shot on the line instead of the bait when using hempseed, elongated split-shot called 'mouse-droppings' are available.

An old-fashioned lead that still finds a use in float-fishing is the barleycorn, a streamlined bored-through weight used in conjunction with a large float where a long cast is required.

Legers include the drilled bullet, an elongated version of this called a barrel, coffin leads, which are flat, slightly elongated, octagonal weights, with swivels at each end, designed to resist rolling; the Arlesey bomb, a pear-shaped casting weight with a swivel at the narrow end, invented by Richard Walker; and the Wye lead, a slightly banana-shaped weight with swivels, designed to resist rolling in fast water conditions.

The spiral lead is used above lightweight lures to keep them low in the water, and anti-kink leads fold over the line above spinners or spoons, to prevent the lures imparting twist to the line.

For sea-fishing, heavier weights are required to resist the strong forces of tides and other currents. Pyramid leads, and the shallower pyramid capta lead, conical leads, five pointed star, and watch leads are all used for boat fishing, where the tackle is simply lowered over the side.

Those most used for casting are the larger version of the Wye lead, the swivelled bomb (Arlesey type), torpedoes, a much larger drilled bullet, and the streamlined casting lead. Versions of this last and the torpedo, have wire 'spraggs' that dig into the sea-bed when extra holding power is needed.

The plummet is a conical lead that is not used for fishing, but for ascertaining the depth of water being fished.

The hook is passed through the eye at the top, then stuck into the cork let into the base, and the tackle is cast to the required spot, and the float is adjusted on the line until the optimum position is found.

Continental leads are making inroads into Britain, mainly the very small types becoming familiar. Such names as Paquita, a small bomb-shaped lead with a fine hole bored through for lightweight lines, the similar Torpille, and the cylindrical Styl leads are to be found in tackle shops.

Moulds are obtainable for casting lead weights at home, but this is a practice that, although producing weights far cheaper than are commercially available, should not be embarked upon lightly, as it involves dealing with molten metals, which can be dangerous. The lead, fairly easily obtainable in pipe form, is melted in a crucible (an iron or steel container) – a blow lamp will produce enough heat for this – and poured into the moulds.

These are usually of aluminium, occasionally of brass, and should be held firmly in a vice.

The moulds should be heated before use, as this prevents distortion and leakage, and gets rid of any moisture, which, if present can cause spitting as it turns instantly to trapped steam, with sometimes painful results.

Any wires, swivels, or spraggs that need to be incorporated should be inserted before the lead is poured. The moulds can be 'struck' or opened after a few minutes cooling time, and the lead removed.

If casting more than one batch, allow the moulds to cool a little after each casting. Wear thick gloves when handling the mould or the crucible.

lead-cored line – a very fast-sinking wet-fly line, used by trolling across a lake or reservoir with a fly, to tempt big, bottom-feeding trout.

lead link – a wire loop designed to allow for the quick changing of weights on a paternoster or boom type of tackle.

Used by sea-fishermen, the loop's end passes around its standing part without being closed off, allowing weights to be slipped on and off easily. Usually linked to an eye.

leader – the business end of a fly line, also called a cast, a length of nylon attached to the line at one end, and the fly at the other.

The leader can be anything from 3 to 5 metres long (9 to 15ft), and is tapered, either by knotting on lengths of lighter line, or using a knotless taper. Americans use the term for any trace or cast.

leather carp – an almost scaleless specimen of the common carp *cyprinus carpio*, carrying just a few scales on the caudal peduncle and at the base of the dorsal fin, and occasionally near other fins. The lateral line has become a shallow, narrow furrow.

leger – to leger has come to mean fishing with the bait on the bottom, without benefit of a float, with a weight to hold the line in one place, and some method of monitoring movement on the line at the rod.

However, the leger was originally the name for the weight, through which the line was free to move when the fish had taken the bait.

Legers (the weights, that is) take many different shapes and sizes, depending on the conditions in which they are used, ranging from a simple straight-through drilled bullet with a single hook used in still waters, to heavy capta or pyramid leads holding down several hooked traces on a paternoster.

There are also tackles that utilise a bubble float or floats a little above the paternoster to hold it up in the water to present the bait attractively. Legering is used in fresh-water and sea fishing, particularly where a long cast is required, in order to fish a long way away from the bank or shore, and it is one of the easiest methods to use from a boat, where a weighted line is simply dropped over the side, using a short rod.

See also Wye leads, torpedo, coffin, Kilmore boom, French boom, weights and leads.

leger stop – a device to stop the leger from sliding down the line, usually a short length of plastic or brass tubing with a tapering bung, which traps the line.

legislation – freshwater anglers are restricted by national laws governing the times of year at which they may fish for certain types of fish (supposedly tied in with the spawning season), licence fees for the use of the rod, and local permits (usually linked to a fee).

Byelaws in some areas vary fishing seasons, ban the use of some tackles and baits, and there may be size limits and restrictions on the numbers of fish to be taken, particularly in some trout fisheries.

Permits and licences should be carried on the person, as the water bailiff is unlikely to allow you to carry on fishing on the promise that you will bring them next time. He will at least insist that you stop fishing, and may even confiscate your tackle.

Sea-fishermen are far less restricted – no licences are required, but there may be local byelaws about beachcasting on crowded beaches at the height of the holiday season, and permission may have to be obtained to fish off some piers, groynes, or harbour walls (very occasionally this will involve a fee).

Fishing from a boat carries with it only the restrictions to which a boat is liable, and these are usually only concerned with safety – you don't really want to hang around down-range in an artillery practice area.

lemon sole – *microstumus kitt,* an oval-shaped flatfish that prefers muddy sea-beds, feeding in the summer months on marine worms and soft crabs, both of which prove to be good baits.

Caught commercially all around the British Isles, these fish are found up to 2kg (4.4lb), and are good to eat, featuring on restaurant menus when the dover sole is too expensive.

lesser spotted dogfish – *scyliorhinus raninculus,* a member of the shark family, also known as the common dogfish, or the rough hound.

By its name, smaller than the greater spotted dogfish, it grows to about 2kg (4.4lb), and has brown spots.

All the dogfish are edible, with a somewhat soft flesh, and are popular with the public as they have very few bones. Known in fish-and-chip shops euphemistically as 'rock salmon'.

lice – *argulus foliaceus,* a small parasitic, blood-sucking crustacean that clings to some freshwater fish.

lift-bite – some fish, instead of taking the baited hook away from the angler, will rise towards the surface with it, lifting the weighted line so that the float, instead of dipping below the surface, rises or even lies flat on the water.

lily pads – the large floating leaves of the water lily are of interest to the angler for two reasons – fish lurk beneath them, and, if a fishing line is cast so that it lies across the leaves, there is no tell-tale trace on the water's surface.

Limerick hook – a sea-fishing hook which curves more abruptly towards the point, in the same way as a crystal hook. This gives good penetration, owing to the angle of the point, and a firm hold. Good for general bottom fishing.

limpets – a conical shaped shell-fish that clings to rocks. Prised loose, the meat of these make good bait.

line bites – indications of bites caused by fish accidentally bumping into a legered line.

Experience enables the angler to differentiate between these and real bites. This phenomenon is mostly experienced when a shoal of fish is feeding around your line, so if troubled by a number of these occurrences, move your bait so that it is on the near edge of your groundbait pattern, or upstream of it if fishing a stream.

line coding – the classification of fly lines according to the AFTM (Association of Fishing Tackle Manufacturers). *See fly lines.*

line guard – a wire or sheet-metal shield over a portion of the open part of a centre-pin reel, put there to stop loose line falling off the reel, and causing a tangle.

line retrieval ratio – the gearing of a fishing reel. A multiplier reel with a ratio of 1:3 will wind line in three times as fast as a centre-pin reel with no gearing, which will have a ratio of 1:1.

line shadow – on a bright day a fishing line, floating on the surface of the water, casts a shadow that can cause fish to jump over the line as if there were a wall in the water.

This can be obviated when legering by sinking the line, and when fly-fishing by using a line that floats in the surface film rather than on top of the water – this throws a smaller shadow.

line twist – the enemy of the angler because it eventually weakens and ruins the line, line twist can be caused by several sets of circumstances.

One hybrid type of reel, a centre-pin that can swing round to become a fixed spool reel for casting purposes, throws the line out with the twist imparted by winding it on the reel, then retrieves it with the wrong bias, twisting it even more. Spinning, or using any lure that twist the line, gives the same trouble, but this can be avoided or obviated by the use of swivels and anti-kink leads or vanes.

ling – *molva molva,* a member of the cod family, and resembling the cod, except that it has a longer body, and long dorsal and anal fins.

A deepwater fish, the ling likes to hang around in the weeds surrounding wrecks or reefs, where it is a voracious feeder on many kinds of smaller fish. It falls prey to squid heads or whitebait, or lasks of freshly caught mackerel, and is occasionally taken on pirks or feathers.

Found all around Britain except, for some obscure reason, the central part of the Channel, the best being taken in the clear waters off Cornwall and the southern coast of Ireland.

Growing to some size – around 20kg (44lb), it resembles the cod in flavour as well as appearance, and in fish and chip shops in some parts of the British Isles is preferred to its cousin.

link leger – a form of leger tackle consisting of a swivel/spring link/weight combination, with an eye above the swivel, through which the line is passed, with a stopper shot or shots limiting the travel of the leger up and down the line.

This arrangement allows for more sensitivity of contact between the rod and the bait or the bite, and if the weight should sink in soft mud, saves the line from being buried.

link swivel – a swivel, incorporating a clip resembling the clip on a dog lead, to which a weight is attached. *See also snap link.*

littoral – of or on the shore: close to the sea: also, the area of the shore between high and low water marks of spring tides.

Be it sandy, muddy, rocky or weed-strewn, this is the prime place for the sea-angler to find his baits – crabs, marine worms, mussels, limpets, sandeels, prawns, etc.

All of these and more can be found with a little diligence, and, of course, fished on the rising tide when fish are coming in looking for just these delicacies.

The area of the littoral varies with geographical location and physical peculiarities. In confined seas such as the Mediterranean, the rise and fall of the tide is very small, about 30cm (1ft) or so, while in other areas the range between low and high tides can be over 12m (40ft).

Furthermore, a steeply shelving beach will give a narrow littoral, while a shallow slope leaves a wide expanse uncovered at low tide – indeed, a combination of a shallow sloping beach and a large tidal range can give a littoral a mile wide.

Beware when beachcasting at low tide on such a beach unless you know the beach and the tidal flow well. A seemingly flat beach can undulate, and many an angler has been cut off by the tide racing up a previously unseen valley behind him, and sand or mud, firm in the sun, can become a shifting, quaking morass when wet.

Bear in mind also that the tide can move at an alarming rate – in Morecambe Bay, for instance, the tide comes in faster than a horse can gallop.

live-baiting – using a live small fish as bait for larger, predatory fish. As the bait-fish is under some physical restraint, and some psychological pressure, it acts like a sick fish, and presents itself as an easy meal.

The tackle and rod selected should be of sufficient strength to cast the size of bait used, and to deal with the class of fish you are after.

The least cruel method of affixing the bait seems to be the simple large hook through the lip – hopefully the bait will get away when the predator is hooked – but this method is not too secure, as the bait can fly off when cast, or, with larger baits, work its way off the hook.

A snap-tackle obviates this problem. Snap-tackles consist of a wire trace with a treble terminal, and one or two trebles arranged to slide freely along the trace.

The terminal treble can be hooked into the bait's lip, with the others hooked into its back, or alternatively, the terminal can be hooked into the underbody of the bait-fish, and the trace wound around it, the other hooks embedded to keep it in place. The rest of the tackle can consist of a simple through-leger, a paternoster, or float tackle.

Are you grilling fish? Turn to page 68 for some culinary guidance. *Bon appetit!*

loach – two species of loach are found, the stone loach *noemacheilus barbatula* and the spined loach *cobiti taenia*.

They are similar, both being of a mottled brown colour, and the most obvious difference is that the spined loach has a flatter head, with a spine below each eye – the spine can prick if the fish is handled clumsily, but the wound is usually harmless.

Both fish have six barbels around the mouth, two of those of the stone loach being longer, those on the spined loach being all the same length.

These barbels are the prime method of differentiation between loach, young barbel, and gudgeon, which have only two and four respectively.

Another distinction is that the tiny scales of these fish do not overlap, but lie flat next to each other.

As the loach grow only to about 12 - 18 cm (5 - 7 in), they are mostly of interest as bait-fish, used live or dead, but apparently the flesh of the stone loach has its devotees as a gourmet dish.

There is a further loach, common on the European continent, called the pond loach, or weather-fish, *misgurnis fossilis*. It is a popular bait-fish for catfish, barbel, etc.

loading a reel – fishing line comes on plastic spools, and has to be wound on to the reel. With the old-fashioned centre-pin reel, this presents no problems except for the method of securing the line to the reel – it is unlikely that all the line will be taken out by a fish, but if it is, and the end is not secured properly, it will slip round the spindle, and the hapless angler can wind away all night without bringing it back.

As reels vary, it is up to the individual to find the answer to this particular conundrum.

Multiplier reels usually have some means of fixing, and as they are wound straight, like the centre-pin, present no twist problems. However, fixed spool reels do have an inherent fault, because they dispense line at right-angles to the line of cast.

When the bale arm is opened, the line slips off in coils instead of coming straight off. This imparts a twist to the line, which is not assisted when the line is retrieved, as it is laid down in the same direction, giving more twist.

This situation can be obviated to some degree when the line is wound on to the reel.

Instead of pushing a pencil through the plastic spool and winding it off straight, fix, or have someone hold, the spool at right-angles to the direction of take-off, so that the line spills over the flange in the same way as it does off the reel.

This will ensure that the line is given an opposite twist, which will unwind when the line is cast.

lobworms – the largest earthworm found in the British Isles (as opposed to marine worms), the lobworm is found near the surface in wet weather, going deeper in dry or cold conditions.

Although easily found by digging, they can be found with less effort on the surface on dewy nights with the aid of a torch or lamp – the lawn is the best place to find them. They are easily kept in containers with some soil and/or leaf-mould, and it makes sense to store supplies for those days when cold or dry weather prevents collection.

The lobworm can be used whole when after large fish, or cut or broken up into smaller pieces for smaller fish.

They are best used on a largish hook, and hooked through the tough, smooth ring around the middle called the clittelum, the egg-case.

If this is not present, the worm is called a 'maiden', and can be hooked anywhere, but is perhaps best twice-hooked.

loch – a lake in Scotland and Ireland, where it is spelt lough. Lochs, or lochan in Scotland, are primarily game fishing preserves, sea-lochs and those that are part of a river system holding salmon, sea-trout and trout, while the smaller highland lochs will hold small trout and char.

Although coarse fish are not much found in Scotland, some lochs hold pike, which are the bane of the game fisherman.

Irish loughs do have coarse fish; rudd, roach, bream, perch and occasionally tench will be found, but the game fish predominate.

loggerhead – colloquial name for the chub.

long belly – a variation on the forward taper or weight forward line used in fly-fishing, where the weight necessary to cast a light fly is in the forward end of the line.

long-distance casting – mostly practised when beachcasting, this has become a sport in itself, tournaments being held in which phenomenal distances are reached.

Aerodynamic weights like the Arlesey bomb or torpedo leads are used, up to 0.25kg (10oz) in weight.

The introduction of carbon-fibre in rods has meant that even the average angler is casting 146 to 164m (160-180 yds) and we look forward to the day when 228 to 274m (250 to 300 yds) is the norm.

long-trotting – a method of float-fishing in which the float and bait are cast upstream and allowed to drift down-stream through a swim, line being paid out gradually.

Most anglers prefer a centre-pin reel for this, pulling off as much line as required, but it can be done with a fixed spool reel, allowing line to slip off, controlled by a fingertip.

loop to loop knot – a method of attaching a leader to a fly-line, in which the fly-line has a whipped loop made with a needle knot in its end, and the leader has a loop at the butt end made with an overhand knot or a blood bight.

The two loops are then overlapped, and the leader loop is pulled halfway through the other, and the leader end pulled through the resulting loop.

loose feeding – groundbaiting an area with frequently thrown small amounts of food, such as maggots or hempseed. If the area you wish to bait is too far for throwing, a baitdropper is useful.

low water – low tide, or, in a river, lake or reservoir, the state of the water during a drought.

lugworm – *arenicola marina*, a marine worm that is easily found on sandy or mud beaches from the 'cast' it leaves behind when burrowing, just like an earthworm.

When these are found, a short distance away will be a small depression, the blow-hole. The worm will be in a 'U'-shaped tunnel between the two indicators, a foot or so down. Take a flat-tined fork (thin tines break the worms, and spades cut them up) and a non-galvanised container, and if the worms are numerous, dig as one would in the garden, turning the worms up like potatoes.

If they are few and far between, the sand between the blow-hole and the cast must be removed, and the worm tracked down.

The non-galvanized container is important, as zinc kills lugworms. Store the lugworms in damp newspaper, at no higher than 40° F, and they will keep for up to a week.

The common lug-worm, often known as the 'blow lug' to distinguish it from others of the family such as the black lug, is not hermaphrodite but normally sexed male and female. Spawning takes place in late summer, and recovery takes a couple of weeks or so, during which time they seem to disappear, as they do not eat, so cast no casts.

The lugworm, being comparatively large, can be used in pieces for small fish – flatfish particularly, as they have small mouths, but for large fish the whole worm is necessary.

Use the baitholder type of hook, with a sliced shank, piercing the worm at the head, threading it onto the hook. Many species of fish will take the lugworm, but it is most famous for taking cod when cast from the beach.

lumpsucker – *cyclopterus lumpus*, a lumpy fish with a sucker! It uses the sucker on its underside to cling on to rock in fast tidal flows and strong currents.

Also known as the sea hen, varying in colour from yellow in the female to orange in the male, it can grow to a fair size, up to 6kg (13lb), and can be caught on marine worms, crab, and fish bait.

> The roe of this fish is sold as an imitation caviar.

> **luncheon meat** – some brands of canned meat, particularly those of a rubbery texture that stay on the hook well, make good baits. As to flavours, why not experiment?

lures – any non-animate bait could be termed a lure, but the word is usually used to cover items manufactured in wood, plastic or metal, or a combination of these materials, designed to simulate the action of a small fish or other marine life, drawn through the water to give the appearance of weakness or illness, making the fish think that it will be an easy meal.

Into this category come Devon minnows, spinners, plugs, spoons, pirks or jigs, feathers, and many imitation fish (sandeels being a favourite for this).

Colours are important, as is brightness, and strange to say, the most successful colours on dull days and murky waters are not, as would be expected, bright, but dull, while bright colours do best on bright days in clear water.

mackerel – *scomber scombrus,* a member of the tuna family, this fish is readily identified from its torpedo shape, and dark blue marbled back (it occasionally sports a varied colouration such as spotted or scribbled).

The mackerel, which is mostly a surface-feeding fish, is notoriously easy to catch, as they throw themselves at virtually anything that looks as if it might be food with gay abandon – this is a result of the large schools in which they live, as a slow mackerel is a starving mackerel.

Found just about everywhere in British waters in the summer and autumn, they retreat south in the winter, but shoals can still be found during the colder weather in the Channel and off the south west coasts.

While the average weight for a mackerel is around 0.5kg (1lb), there do seem to be a few that reach a good size, over 1.8kg (4lb). Small fish, those in their first year, are called 'joeys'.

It is a favourite rite of the holiday-maker to go out in a hire-boat and catch mackerel on feathers, and, once a shoal is found it is so easy as to become boring after a short while. However, these commercially important fish can give good sport on light tackle, The up-side of the ease of catching mackerel is that they make superb bait for many larger fish, used either whole or cut into lasks.

Where there are mackerel, there are usually shark following the shoals. When fishing for them as bait, the crude methods such as feathers and spinners are permissible.

Mackerel are good to eat, if a little oily. Try them poached in cider, or grilled with a whole-grain mustard sauce!

Cook them well, as they are a reputedly good source of the food-poisoning bacterium clostridium welchii (or clostridium perfringens).

Indeed, not so long ago it was an accepted practice having caught a mackerel with the intention of eating it, to fold over its tail, and cut off the rear part of the body that the tail covered, as this was supposed to be the part where "all this poisons lie".

maddies – small type of ragworm, growing up to 7.5cm (3in), found on muddy beaches, estuaries, etc., and, like the king rag, a burrower.

Maddies live in small colonies, grouped together, and, when dug, are difficult to keep alive for more than a day or so, as they are fairly delicate. Good bait for mullet and garfish.

maggots – the larval stage of various different breeds of fly, primarily the house-fly, the bluebottle, and the greenbottle. Different types of maggots are used, including gozzers, pinkies, and squatts.

In different parts of the British Isles maggots are known by different names, such as hookers, and gentles. Although it is possible to breed maggots for yourself – family allowing – the commercially bred maggot is probably the most used nowadays, and these are often dyed, yellows and orange-coloured being most favoured (many dealers will sell you dyes or anatto paste with which to dye home-grown maggots).

magpie scad fly – a gaudy artificial fly with a harl body and green wings, used to catch sea-trout, especially in deep pools, where its bright colours attract the fish from the deeps.

mako shark – *isurus oxyrhincus*, one of the larger sharks found in British waters, the mako grows to about 205+kg (450-490lb).

A mid-water feeder that prefers the larger fish such as pollack or cod as its main diet, rather than herring or mackerel.

Almost regardless of size, once hooked the mako will give the angler a tremendous fight, part of its repertoire being spectacular leaps clear of the water.

Similar in general shape and size to the porbeagle shark, it is slightly shallower in body-depth at the thickest part of the body, below the dorsal fin, and the tooth pattern in the mako is distinctive, the teeth being long and irregular, whereas in the porbeagle, they are in neat rows.

CULINARY GUIDANCE

Grilled fish

Lightly rub the fish with oil or fat and sprinkle with salt and pepper.

Cut across with three or four deep gashes if it is a whole fish.

Lightly oil the bottom of the grill pan and lay in the fish. Place under a very hot grill.

Small fish or fillets will take 5-10 minutes, larger fish a little longer. Turn mid-way through cooking.

---

malt – barley grains that have been allowed to sprout, usually used in the manufacture of whisky or the brewing of beer, they are good bait for roach, bream, chub, rudd, etc. Hook as for boiled hempseed, although malted grain is usually soft enough to hook without boiling.

---

marbelled trout – a hybrid of the introduced American brook trout *salvelinus fontinalis* (properly a char), and the brown trout *salmo trutta*. The marbelled trout is probably the most beautiful of the salmonidae.

---

mark – when freshwater fishing on a river or small pond it is relatively easy to find the exact same spot you were fishing at a week, month, or year ago, provided you have a good memory or keep some sort of reference system or a diary.

When boat-fishing at sea, however, to return to the same prolific patch of sea is not quite so easy. If within sight of land, bearings can be taken of prominent objects visible on shore, using a hand compass, and these bearings entered on the chart as the 'mark'. This will simplify return.

However, if you are fishing offshore, out of sight of land, the best that can be done is to take a record of your exact course, speed, and the length of time the trip out takes, reinforcing this if possible with an echo-sounder record of the bottom in the immediate area. The outward course can be checked on the return journey – you will need to follow a reciprocal course to get home, anyway!

marlin – the white marlin, *tetrapturus albidus,* a legendary big-game fish, has been sighted in the English Channel, and off the southwest coasts of England, Wales, and Ireland, but none has yet been landed on rod and line in these waters – a record waiting to be set.

marrow spoon – a long, narrow scoop, popular in Victorian times for removing marrow from beef or lamb bones (a delicacy in those days), which can be thrust down the gullet of a newly caught trout to remove the stomach contents for examination (autopsy), in order to determine what the trout has been eating, thus giving an idea what fly/nymph to use to catch more.

Almost a 'Catch-22' situation – if you cannot catch a trout, how can you do the autopsy, and if you have a trout upon which to perform the autopsy, you must have got it right at first guess!

match fishing – fishing in competition, within a club, or between teams from different clubs, or individually in open competitions. Most match fishing takes place over a set time period (usually five hours, but this can vary), and some can have local rules.

match pools – not the water on which fishing matches are staged, but small sweepstakes run as a side bet on the outcome.

match rods – rods made for specific purposes and known conditions, fishing in matches where the types of fish are known, and the tackle used is likely to be light.

Match rods are usually fast-action rods with a fairly soft top-action, which acts as a shock absorber in fast strikes.

matching the hatch – using an artificial fly or nymph that simulates the type of natural flies or larvae that are hatching at any particular time. For instance, it would be pointless using an early summer fly such as the hawthorn in September or October, when the daddy longlegs is hatching, and will be the insect the fish are feeding upon.

margin fishing – a method that has developed over the years to fish for large carp that are known to stalk the marginal waters close to the bank looking for floating particles of food: the bait is lowered gently to float on the surface with no line visible to the fish.

This technique is most effective at night, when the carp follow this particular method of feeding.

marsh worm – a small worm that is found in the mud of pond edges, ditches, canals, etc. About 4 cm (1.5 in) long, red to blue in colour, it is quite delicate, requiring care when hooking, but worthwhile, as many freshwater fish find them irresistible.

mayfly – the largest of the 'dayflies', the mayfly and its larval stages are a popular item of diet with trout in areas in which it is common. Artificial flies and nymphs are made to simulate it, and are used when the fly hatch is under way.

mealworms – not worms, but the grubs and larval stages of a beetle found in flour-milling. Sold in pet-shops as bird food, and food for insect-eating small pets, they can be expensive, but are easy to store in bran or oatmeal.

They are not difficult to breed, being reared from the grub stage to adult in this manner.

meat – many modern canned meats prove to be worthy baits for a wide variety of fish, but be sure to purchase experimental tins before going off on that trip.

Some of the cheaper brands have a high fat content, which makes the meat too soft or friable to stay on the hook, and some of them have an odour that would put off a ravenous wolf!

Luncheon meat, sausage meat, liver sausage (as opposed to 'pate', which is too soft), corned beef, and some petfoods (mostly those prepared for cats, with a fish base) have all proved efficacious in the recent past.

Garlic flavoured sausage seems to be unacceptable. Some sausage meats are a little soft, and may need binding with bread, or mixed with a little egg and lightly cooked.

The high price of these meats usually precludes their use alone as groundbait, but mixed with commercially available cereal groundbait, they go a lot further (both financially, and used with a catapult as a launching medium).

megrim – *lepidorhombus whiffiagonis,* a small deep water flatfish, the megrim is the colour of the sandy bottoms it prefers. Growing to about 1kg (2.2lb), they will take shellfish and worm baits, and are good to eat, being rather like the lemon sole.

mending – when fly-fishing with a greased line, throwing a loop of line by flicking the rod-tip in a small circle. This is done to control the speed with which the fly is moving on the surface, and must be done without the fly being disturbed or the water slapped by the line.

Mepps spoon – a proprietary spoon lure, available in two sizes, good for pike, perch, trout, and salmon.

Mevagissey – an artificial eel made in plastic, named after the Cornish fishing village and coastal resort.

migration – two types of freshwater fish are involved in migration – the salmonidae family, including their cousins, the chars – and the eels.

Salmon and sea-trout migrate to the sea in order to find greater supplies of food, and return to the headwaters of the river of their birth in order to spawn.

Eels, spawned in the depths of the Atlantic just north of the West Indies, an area known colloquially as the 'Sargasso Sea', do not so much swim as float on the currents of the Gulf Stream to the East coast of America and the Western and southern coasts of Europe.

Ascending the rivers, they spread out through the water systems of these continents, using ditches and dew-wet fields to reach even isolated ponds.

After a few years – as much as ten or a dozen – for some unknown reason they decide it is time for them to spawn, and they set out on what is a true migration, all the way back to the Sargasso Sea.

Whether any of the European eels ever make it is unknown – it is thought that all the young that migrate to Europe are the progeny of the eels that live in American waters, who have a short, less hazardous journey.

Many marine fish migrate in an annual pattern, seeking warmer or colder water, according to species. Cod move north in the summer, looking for cooler water, while mackerel move south in winter, looking for warmth.

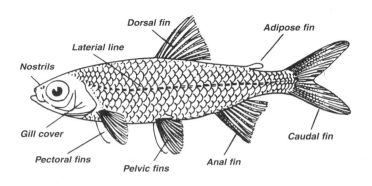

miller's thumb – *cottus gobio,* also known as the bullhead. Of little interest to anglers, except in trout waters, where they are considered undesirable.

minnow – *phoxinus phoxinus,* a tiny fish of the cyprindae that seldom exceeds 10cm (4in), of little interest to anglers except as a bait-fish. The minnow occurs all over Europe, and in many places forms the sole diet of large trout.

Most easily caught by the time-honoured small-boy method of a small net on a stick or in a minnow trap if sought after for bait. The minnow is copied in lure form as the Devon minnow.

minnow trap – a tubular trap made of a transparent plastic, with an inverted conical entry, and a perforated bottom. The trap is placed with its entry facing downstream, and the fish swims in, attracted by small pieces of food inside, and is unable to swim out through the small entry.

mirror carp – a variation of the common carp *cyprinus carpio*, which does not have scales all over its body, but has a few large scales scattered about in irregular patterns on parts of its body, usually near the head, along the back and around the dorsal fin and near the tail, and very occasionally along the lateral line – if found here, they are irregularly placed and usually number fewer than 36.

'Model Perfect' – a brand of fish hook, of reputed great holding power.

mollusc – a soft-bodied animal with a hard shell. This includes such creatures as snails, oysters, cockles, mussels, limpets, and razorfish, all of which make good bait when removed from the shell.

Mona's scale – a scale that gives an approximate weight for a given length of the pike.

monkey climber – a proprietary bite indicator that involves a plastic sliding device that is fitted to the rod.

monkfish – *squatina squatina,* also called the angel fish, although not by aquarium owners.

This is an ugly fish related to the shark family, resembling a halfway point between shark and skate, with two pairs of wing-like fins, a flattened body, a shark-like tail, and it prefers deep water.

It has, like other members of its family, an 'anterior' mouth, that is, set under the head, and it feeds on the bottom on small crustacea, small fish, and molluscs. Growing to a good size – up to 30kg (66lb), with an average about 18-20kg (40 to 45lb) – strong tackle is needed to deal with it.

Opinions as to the monkfish's fighting spirit vary, but few have been caught deliberately. As this fish has been bruited about as possessing very tasty flesh (said to have a flavour akin to scampi), this may change. If so, the west coast of Ireland would seem to be the best place to try, as consistent catches of this odd-looking fish have been made there.

monofilament – literally, single strand. Fishing lines used to be made of braided (plaited) silk, flax, or cotton; these needed considerable maintenance in the form of drying and oiling, and were not conducive to long casting.

Hook lengths or casts were made of gut, and needed careful, handling, as it could be brittle. With the invention in the 1930s of nylon, a synthetic fibre with long-chain molecules, which could be drawn out to a very fine single strand with high tensile strength, most of the problems associated with the old lines could be overcome.

However, although nylon monofilament has many advantages over the old materials, it is not entirely free from faults itself. It absorbs water, which can reduce its advertised breaking strain, and it is affected by the ultra-violet in sunlight.

Furthermore, it is elastic, which contributes to its strength, but is a drawback when it comes to striking, as the shock of the quick rod movement is dissipated as it travels to the fish by this stretchiness.

Also, this elasticity causes any line wound onto the reel with a weight (a fish, or just leger weights) to be wound on with an inbuilt stretch, so that after a day's fishing it needs to be transferred to another reel and wound back under zero tension.

Lastly, nylon monofilament is smooth, so tends to slip when tied with knots that would hold other fibres – the blood knot, the half-blood, the water knot, the double-grinner, and the needle knot are the best methods of securing nylon.

REMEMBER

Nylon is not bio-degradable – it does not decay and return to dust.

If discarded at the water's edge, that is where it will stay, and even a short length can be a hazard to small animals and birds.

Take it home, or burn it.

---

mountain streams – most mountain streams in the British Isles are westerly-flowing, with short, violent courses, and contain mainly trout, which, in these extreme conditions, do not grow very large – 1 to 2kg (2 to 4lb), occasionally up to 3kg (6lb).

The miller's thumb or bullhead is also found in such streams, and is a nuisance where the trout are valued, as it competes for food with the trout young.

These streams are usually fished in the intermittent pools that occur along their lengths, the fly being used only where the pool is large enough, worm fishing often being the only practical method in the small pools.

mud – the condition of the sea- or river-bottom over which you are fishing needs consideration, particularly in view of the type of weight to be used when legering.

Soft, muddy ground will necessitate the use of flat leads, which, although not so efficient in the casting, sink more slowly than streamlined weights which hit the bottom harder, and can sink into the ooze. A flat weight also spreads the load over a larger area.

Best weight for these conditions include the capta lead, the circular grip (also known as the watch weight), and the six-pointed star.

mullet – although both called 'mullet', the red mullet and the grey mullet (both described elsewhere in this book) are not closely related, indeed, they belong to quite different species.

The red mullet is found off the south and southwest coasts of England and Ireland, and occasionally off the east coast of Scotland.

It is more common in the Mediterranean, where it has had a reputation since Roman times for its tastiness – the smoked roe is used for the Greek delicacy taramasalata.

multiplier reel – a centre-pin reel in which the drum or spool is geared at a ratio of 3:1 or 4:1, so that one rotation of the handle give 3 or 4 rotations at the drum, thus enabling fast retrieval of the line.

A line distributor in the shape of a moving gate geared to the winding mechanism is usually incorporated, as are a star-drag, which acts like a clutch, and, sometimes, a brake. The multiplier is usually available only as a right-handed reel, and is mostly used on top of, instead of underneath, the rod.

The drawbacks involved in the use of this type of reel are the need for constant maintenance in the form of dismantling and cleaning, as they are prone to jamming if dirt encroaches into the mechanism, and the infamous 'bird's nest' resulting from over-run when casting or lowering heavy tackle.

This last is supposed to be obviated by the inclusion of star-drags and brakes, but still occurs, and can be overcome by thumb-pressure on the line as it is paid out.

murderer – a sea-angling lure/hook combination consisting of a plastic or metal body about 10cm (4in) long, with two rings of barbs at one end. Used like a jig or pirk, it is very effective in squid fishing.

mussels – both salt-water and freshwater mussels make excellent baits, in, of course, their own habitats. They are easy enough to pull off the rocks to which they anchor themselves, but a sharp knife will be needed to open them and remove the meat (including the toughest part that holds the animal in its shell, which gives a good hook-hold).

There are twenty-eight species of freshwater mussels, of which only the five largest are of use as bait; the swan mussel, *anodonta cygnesis* the largest, growing up to 20cm (8in) across; the painters mussel, *unio pictorum* (the shell was used as a paint container) grows to 13cm (5in); the duck mussel, *anodonta anatina* to about 18cm (7in); the zebra mussel *dreissena polymorpha* up to 5cm (2 in), (this is the closest related to the marine mussels); and the pearl mussel, *margaritfera margaritfera* up to 11cm (4in) across – check for your fortune before using the meat of this one!

There are eight species of marine mussel around the British Isles. The common mussel and the horse mussel are the most used for bait.

Salt-water mussels do not grow to the large sizes reached by freshwater species – probably because they are always getting eaten – and are often used several at a time on the hook.

On the east coast they are tied together onto the hook with a length of wool, or placed into a fine hair-net and hooked on.

nasling – *chondrostoma nasus,* an elegant, slender fish found in Central Europe, in the rivers that feed the Baltic and the North Sea, and in the Danube.

A vegetarian, feeding mostly on algae, which it grazes from stones and rocks in clear-watered streams and lakes, it is a commercially valuable fish in the areas where it is abundant, and is popular with continental anglers, fished on light tackle.

needle flies – slender-bodied flies found locally throughout the British Isles.

needle knot – knot used to attach a leader or a backing line to a fly-line. The thinner nylon monofilament line is pulled through the blunt end of the fly-line with a needle, then whipped to and fro, and finished off with a coat of varnish or whipping filler, giving a smooth join that will not foul rod-rings.

nets – the two nets that the angler will use are the landing net and the keep net.

The first should be wide enough at the mouth to accommodate the largest fish you can expect to catch, with a stout handle, preferably one that can have an extending piece screwed into the butt.

The keep net should have large, soft spacer rings and be long enough to keep your catch in without overcrowding. Both types of net should be of a material that will not harm the fish – the old knotted sort that scraped the scales off the fish are no longer acceptable, and should be destroyed.

neutral density lines – a modern fly-line that acts like the old-fashioned silk fly-line, that is, sinks slowly, unless treated with a floatant.

new scale – a range of hook sizes introduced by Pennell's, which had no correlation with the previously used Redditch scale, and caused much confusion.

N. F. A. – National Federation of Anglers - the national body to which most angling clubs in the British Isles are affiliated.

Their address is – Halliday House, Egginton Junction, Derbyshire DE65 6GU, and the telephone number is 01283 734735.

N. F. S. A. – National Federation of Sea Anglers, the national body that looks after the interests of sea anglers.

Address – 51a Queen Street, Newton Abbott, Devon, TQ12 2QT, and the telephone number is 01626 331330.

night fishing – the main difficulty in fishing at night is that it is dark, so methods that rely on vision are fairly well precluded, unless you want to sit on a river bank with a torch beam directed onto your float tip.

Legering, with an audible bite indicator or a small light at the rod-tip that gives an indication of movement, is about the only method of coarse fishing viable unless there is a considerable 'hunter's moon'.

Fly-fishing at night, particularly for sea-trout, is a thrilling experience, and good catches are obtainable if a large, light-coloured fly is used, simulating a moth. Bear in mind, too, that fish that would not normally stray there during the day will come into the shallows at night.

Study the area you are going to fish during daylight, getting to know likely swims, the depth of water, good landing spots, and, most important, the route to and from your chosen patch. Be careful when wading, feeling ahead with one foot before placing your whole weight on it, and take short steps, so that your balance is not upset.

> If you have to wade in the dark, remember that smooth, dark water with small ripples is probably deep, and rough, broken water with white caps is more likely to be shallow.

In or out of the water, you will want to move slowly to avoid disturbing the fish – this has an added bonus of being safer.

When beach-casting at night, bear in mind that if the tide is out, it is as well to know the terrain of the beach, and the action of the tide in the area, to avoid being cut off – this applies also when fishing from rocks.

Norway pout – *trisopterus esmarkii*, a small member of the cod family, closely related to the whiting, this fish grows up to about 20cm (8in) in length.

Similar in most respects to its cousin, it has a proportionately larger eye than the whiting. Like the other pouting, it is remarkably easy to catch, taking almost any bait, although it prefers crustaceans. It is found in the North Sea, around the north coast of Scotland, and down the west coasts of Scotland, England, and Ireland.

Nottingham slider – a cork-bodied goose-quill float with slider rings.

nylon – the largest single advance in tackle since the inception of fishing as a sport has been the invention of nylon, a synthetic polymer fibre originally intended as a replacement for silk in its many uses.

Fishing lines that were once made of maintenance-demanding silk, linen, or cotton, are now made of nylon monofilament that is almost maintenance-free, translucent, and can be made more accurately at consistent thicknesses and predictable breaking strains.

Also, braided nylon lines are available for those types of fishing for which monofil is unsuitable.

nymph – the larval stages of various aquatic insects, which spend the first part of life in the water, and rise to throw off their nymphal casings above the surface, and become flies. These larvae are food for many fish, and flies are tied to represent them, and fished below the surface to simulate the hatching rise.

occlusion of the stomach – a theory put forward by some authorities for the fact that salmon do not feed while on their upstream journey to spawn.

offshore fishing – properly, offshore means out of sight of land. Marks are difficult to find without geographical reference points from which to take bearings, so take along an expert navigator, or hire a boat with a skipper who knows his local waters.

olivette – a small pear-shaped weight used when float-fishing.

opah – *lampris guttatus,* a brilliantly coloured, deep-bodied fish that is but rarely caught on rod and line in British waters.

Blue over the back, with orange/pink flanks and underside, the whole being spotted with white, this fish can grow to quite a size, over 45kg (100lb). Also known as the moonfish.

> **otter** – a marine mammal that lives on fish, the otter was long hated by anglers, as it depleted fish stocks.
>
> Hunting and loss of habitat has resulted in great loss of numbers of this fascinating animal, which has as much right as humans to eat fish, and it is to be hoped that the otter population will recover.
>
> Also, an otter was a device for recovering tackle snagged underwater.

overcasting – casting too far, past the spot where the bait is required.

overhead cast – a style of casting where the rod is raised straight up and brought backwards over the head, then snapped forwards, pointing at the spot where the tackle should land.

oxygen – the corrosive gas upon which most of life on earth depends; the oxygen content of water governs the types of fish that will live in that water.

Trout demand a high oxygen content, while the tench, for instance, can live in low oxygen conditions.

The oxygen content of water depends on absorption, which is influenced to a degree upon the amount of agitation of the water, so a fast running stream on a rocky bed will have a higher oxygen content than a sluggish river or a still lake.

The sea, being in constant motion, will normally be high in oxygen.

pandora bream – *pagellus erythrinus,* an occasional visitor to the south and west coasts of England, this fish is similar to the red bream, but lacks the large dark spot at the top of its lateral line.

Slightly slimmer than its cousin, it has proportionately larger eyes, but general colouration is the same.

paquita lead – a continental lead, pear-shaped, with a small central hole through it. This lead is fixed on the line either by pinching the narrow end on the line, or using a small shot above and below. Used with very fine tackle.

parr – an early stage in the life of the members of the salmonidae, after the alevin and fry stages. The young fish is a parr from about six months up until about two years, when it becomes a smolt, and starts on its migration downstream.

paste – A bait made from stale bread, which is soaked in water until soft, the excess water being squeezed out and the resultant mush gently kneaded until it is a soft paste, which can be moulded around the hook. Good for roach, bream, tench, chub, carp, and even barbel.

paste bobbin – a lump of bread paste squeezed on the line between the reel, and the first rod-ring, to act as a bite indicator when legering. A loop of line is left dangling with the paste attached, and any disturbance of the bait end of the line is transmitted to the indicator, movement of this being easier to see than the movement of the line.

paternoster – a boom a few inches long, made of wire or plastic, that is hung on a fishing line in order to keep a hook-length or trace from tangling with the main line.

peacock quill float – a delicate float made from a peacock's quill.

peeler crab — a crab that is about to shed its carapace as part of its growth process. Crabs, which are crustacea, being exo-skeletal, can only grow by shedding the old carapace, having grown a new one underneath.

This it does, hiding until the new shell hardens – during this period it is called a 'softback'. Many anglers consider the crab at the peeler stage to be the finest sea-fishing bait available, being especially attractive to bass and cod. Depending on size, the whole crab or just parts, can be used.

pegs – in some competitions, the places on the river or lake bank at which each individual will fish are marked with numbered pegs of wood stuck in the bank. The numbers are drawn out of a hat to ensure impartiality of placing.

Also, refers to the length of river-bank covered by the peg – usually, a peg is about 20 yards.

pelagic – ocean-going. Thus, a pelagic jelly-fish is the large, ocean-travelling type as opposed to the inshore varieties.

pelamid – *sarda sarda,* a small member of the tunny family, an occasional visitor to southern British waters, found mostly further south in the Atlantic, and the Mediterranean. Growing to about 4 to 4.5kg (8.8-9.9lb), it follows mackerel shoals.

> Like all this group, good to eat, and is usually barbecued for the delectation of tourists to the Costa Del Sol.

pellet feeding – modern trout hatcheries feed the growing trout on pelleted feed containing all the protein, fats, carbohydrates, vitamins and minerals necessary for healthy growth. Most also use the earth pond system, which allows the fish to take as a proportion of their diet the natural foods that they would take in nature.

When released into the wild, these fish acclimatise fairly quickly, whereas those fed only on pellets take a while to settle down and find their own food.

pennel tackle – two hook rig used for trout fishing with worms.

perch – *percia fluviatalis,* the leading member of the family percidae in British waters, the perch is happy in almost any habitat, being found in lakes, ponds, rivers, and streams throughout Europe.

The only exception is fast-running cold streams, where it can live, but will not breed.

The perch is easily distinguished, having a deep, slightly hump-backed body, dark green on the back, blending into dark green bars down its flanks, which are bronze or pale green, as is the underside.

The fins are distinctive; there are two dorsal fins, the anterior having hard, sharp spines throughout, the posterior having only a couple of hard spines, the rest being soft.

The fins on the underside are an orange-grey red, as is the tail. The skin is rough, being covered with tough scales, and the gill covers are triangular, with the point of the triangle at the rear being sharp enough to inflict a wound.

The perch is a voracious predator – there is very little it will not attack. When young it is a gregarious fish, living and hunting in large shoals. In these circumstances, with a good supply of food, it will grow to about 2 to 2.5kg (4 to 5lb), overpopulation sometimes restricting growth rates and sizes, although there are records of perch of up to 3.5kg (8lb) being netted in drainage operations.

These large specimens are usually solitary fish, and are seldom caught on rod and line, so there is obviously room in the record books for anyone who takes the large perch seriously. Almost any method of fishing and any meaty bait will catch them, but spinning offers the most fun.

In common with most freshwater fish, the perch is neglected insofar as the kitchen is concerned.

It was not always so – in Victorian times the 'perch breakfast' was fashionable – groups of gentlemen would take frying pans and small primus stoves out on punts on early morning expeditions, and fry and eat the perch they caught.

A firm, white flesh, it rivals that of the trout for flavour, and is best fried, grilled or barbecued.

permits – there are very few places in the British Isles (apart from the sea) where the angler can fish for free. Apart from the National Rivers Authority rod licences, which must be obtained (available at tackle shops and Post Offices), there are invariably local permits to be purchased from whichever authority or club administers the waters in that area.

These may be obtainable at the tackle shops, Post Offices, Tourist Information Offices, or collectable by bailiffs at the waterside.

Some trout fisheries charge by the day and allow only a set number if fish are to be taken.

Bear in mind also that, the sea apart, there are set close seasons during which no fishing is allowed, and these may vary from district to district.

phantom – a type of spinner.

pharyngeal teeth – teeth set in the throat, usually bearing against the upper, hard palate. The lack of teeth in the mouth is generally an indication that the fish is not a predator, but even vegetarians have to have some way of grinding up their food, hence the pharyngeal teeth. The cyprynid family have them, as do wrasses.

pickers – small codling in their first and second years.

pick-up – also known as the bale arm – the wire loop that retrieves the line on a fixed-spool reel.

piers – the sea-side pier is almost entirely a British phenomenon, brought about during the Victorian era, when pleasure steamers plied our coasts, taking the tripper to resorts that lacked natural harbours.

The piers were built out to fairly deep water, where the vessels could approach without fear of grounding (the pier at Southend, in Essex, was 2 Km (1.25 miles) long, and boasted an electric railway to save passengers the walk).

As the first place the incoming tripper would visit, the pier soon grew into a place of amusement itself, the sooner to fleece the tourist, and licensed bars were soon common. However, the local populations soon realised that there was another type of amusement to be had at the end of the pier.

As they were built into fairly deep water, it meant that fish were readily accessible without the risks or expense of taking to a boat, or strenuously casting from the beach. Relatively safe for youngsters to fish from, and learn the use of their tackle without the need to cast, with the companionship of several other anglers alongside, and the shelter of the buildings and windbreaks in inclement weather, the piers offered an ideal platform, and many a fine bass was taken on Brighton's piers. The types of fish to be caught off piers will vary around the coast, but there are several that will not be caught by the sea-going angler – the grey mullet among them.

There is one drawback in fishing from piers. They were invariably built of cast iron, and the landing stages and fishing areas were floored from this material in a grid pattern. This was probably a sensible idea, allowing water to drain through in wet weather, but anyone who has ever caught an eel from such a pier will know just how bad a bird's nest this fish can make of your tackle by squirming down one hole, up another, down another, and so on. Have a newspaper ready to lay him on!

pike – *esox lucius,* also known as the luce, and when young as a jack, the only European representative of the family esocidae, the common pike earns its sobriquet of 'the wolf of the waters'.

It is designed and built with one purpose – predation. The long slender camouflaged body, mottled or barred brown or green, is muscular and streamlined, built for the quick dash from ambush. The wide, bill-like mouth is full of small, needle-sharp teeth that are fused with the jaw-bones, and slope backward to act as barbs, not allowing the prey to escape.

The eyes are so arranged as to give binocular vision over a wide frontal area, whereas most fish have a very small area of binocular sight, each eye covering a large separate area to the side and rear. This fish looks like a wolf!

Pike fishing can become an obsession with anglers, to the exclusion of all else. Devotees will sit on a bleak river-bank in the depths of winter – a favourite time for masochistic pike fishermen, who have convinced themselves that winter is preferable to summer for their sport, and pike fishing is even banned by some clubs until after October.

The reason for this obsession is that the pike fisherman stands the best chance of a specimen fish, as these beasts can grow to 27kg (60lb) or more, and, being powerful fish, fight like fury when hooked.

In winter-time, food is scarcer, the pike is hungrier, and also leaner, fitter, and more likely to give a good fight.

Found in almost all slow-running waters, lakes, ponds, and reservoirs in Britain, and throughout Europe with the exceptions of Spain, southern Italy, and parts of the Balkans, the pike can be caught on almost any fish bait, including the young of its own species, and with herring, mackerel, sprats, and prawns, and on almost every type of spinning lure or plug.

The now discredited method of live-baiting has largely given way to the use of dead-bait, but whatever method is chosen, it is best to fish on the margins of the river or lake, near the weed-beds in which the pike likes to lurk, or on the edges of shoals of the small fish upon which it preys.

If possible, watch for the areas avoided by the duck and moorhen, for the pike will take these, and any small mammal such as water vole.

Before the salmon became popular on English tables, the pike was the delicacy of note, especially at Tudor banquets – Henry VIII was said to be partial to a darne of pike!

A rich, creamy-white meat, it is best baked, served with a tangy sauce.

pike-perch – 1. *stizostedian lucioperca,* and 2. *stizostedian vitreum,* the zander and the wall-eye, are both introduced fish, the first brought from Europe by the Duke of Bedford in the early part of the twentieth century, and the second from the Americas.

They are so similar that they may, for all intents and purposes, be regarded as the same species, and both are related to the eastern pike-perch *stizostedian volgense,* from which the European variety at least is descended, travelling westwards at the end of the last Ice Age. Presumably others travelled eastwards to the North American continent.

Not related to the pike, definitely not a hybrid, they are members of the percidae, and share the fin layout and the colouration of the perch, except for the orange on the lower fins, but are more elongated and streamlined.

As predatory as its cousin, the pike-perch can grow to a considerable size – 5kg (11lb) is quite normal, and 13+kg (30lb) has been recorded on the continent.

After several introductions since the Noble Duke's efforts, they are found throughout East Anglian waters, and fished with all the normal methods employed against perch, they give a good fight when hooked.

Most fish baits will take them, but they are reputed to be a touch sluggish, and uninterested in spinners or spoons. Reputed, like the other members of their family, to be good to eat.

pilchard – *sardina pilchardus,* a fish once prolific in southwestern waters of the British Isles (the famous 'Stargazey pie' from Cornwall consisted of pilchards in a pie with their heads looking upwards, piercing the crust).

Growing only to 15 to 20cm (6 to 8in), the pilchard is seldom caught on rod and line and is only of interest to the angler insofar as it is an important food-fish.

Larger fish, including shark, follow the pilchard shoals, which have now unfortunately diminished in size and frequency through commercial overfishing.

The pilchard makes a very good bait, and pilchard oil, if available, is the best for bait injection or dipping.

> From the numbers of pilchards sold in cans, it is obviously very palatable – if you should catch any, they are best gently barbecued, where their oiliness makes them self-basting.

pilot float – a sliding secondary float above the mainfloat, used when pike-fishing with livebait. As the pike takes the bait from the side, then, having taken it to its lair, or just into deeper water, shifts it to be swallowed head-first.

With a lip-hooked bait fish, it is obviously pointless to strike while the bait is sideways on, and the hook nowhere near the mouth. The pilot float shows when the pike has stopped this short trip, and the skilled angler can gauge just when to strike.

pinkies – the maggot or larva of the greenbottle fly. Smaller than the maggot of the bluebottle, it is used, like the housefly maggot or squatt, as a feeder, that is, as a groundbait thrown in to attract fish, which will then be delighted to find a nice big gozzer lying among them.

The pinkie can be used as hook-bait on the occasion that fine tackle, tiny hook, and small bait is called for.

pinnacle fishing – submerged rocky pinnacles, the existence of which will be well-known to any local boatman or skipper, are ideal places to fish with the pirk or jig.

Cod, ling, and pollack favour these areas, and conger lurk in holes and crevices on them.

piper – *trygla lyra,* a member of the gurnard family, of similar colouration to the red gurnard, it is slightly tubbier, growing to 1.5kg (3lb). Differentiation can be made by the contours of the lateral line, which is serrated in the red gurnard, smooth in the piper.

pirk – a lure consisting of curved, coloured weight, usually with a triple hook at its lower end. Many types are available commercially, but they are also quite easily made at home.

Mostly used, like jigs, for wreck fishing, cast and retrieved quickly, using a multiplier reel. Very effective as a lure, the weight of the pirk means that a good deal of a fighting fish's energy is overcome in its tussle with it, rather than with the angler.

plaice – *pleuronectes platessa,* a middling sized flatfish of the order heterosomata, which means 'twisted body', referring to their habit of swimming along on one side of their flattened bodies.

In great demand commercially, the plaice prefers shallow waters, and sandy or gravelly bottoms, where it can utilise its legendary camouflage techniques (it can change colour to blend in with its surroundings).

The upper body is of varying shades of brown, with spots that vary from bright orange to deep red. The underside is a bluey/white.

Growing to about 3kg (6.6lb), it takes marine worms, small crustacea, razor fish, bivalves, and is found all around the British Isles. Mostly caught on leger tackle using shellfish, but will also take spinning lures – a spoon baited with small fish or strips of fish gives good sport. Although it is known that plaice eat lugworm and ragworm, these are not so successful as bait.

> The plaice has quite a strong flavour, which is enhanced through frying – for a milder result, try poaching, with a little dry white wine in the liquor, making the poaching liquid into a sauce with a little cheese, or including a few thinly sliced mushrooms.

plasticizer – the plastic used to coat modern fly lines is PVC – polyvinyl chloride – is a hard, brittle plastic, and has a plasticizer added during manufacture in order to soften it, and make it pliable.

Unfortunately, plasticizers have a habit of leeching out over time and with use, leaving the line brittle and unusable. This can be obviated to a degree by the use of a plasticizing grease on the line, so although modern materials usually lessen the amount of maintenance needed, it is not always the case.

playing fish – the art of getting the hooked fish to the shore, gaff, or landing net.

By the judicious use of the clutch or brake on the reel, rod angle, and knowledge of the waters being fished, it is possible to land a heavy fish on light tackle, with a line of far lower breaking strain than the weight of the fish.

The general idea is to tire the fish, not allowing it to get into weed or any other underwater obstacle.

Many pages in many books have, and will be, written on this subject, but fish still get away. There is no substitute for experience.

plugs – a range of lures, made of wood, plastic, or metal, designed to imitate the movements of small prey, fish or animals.

There are floating plugs which represent water shrews or mice, or sick fish, diving plugs that dip below the water when retrieved, sinking plugs, deep divers, plugs for pike, plugs that wiggle, plugs with tassels – all manner and flavours of plug.

plummet lead – a lead weight with a cork bottom and a fixed loop at the top.

The hook is threaded through the loop, and stuck into the cork. This is then used to try the depth of the water to be fished, and some plummets have a plasticine lump on the bottom to give an indication of the type of bottom – sand, mud, gravel, etc.

point – as a fly line is quite a heavy, thick piece of equipment, the fly is not tied directly to it, as it would frighten the fish when it lands on the water.

A 'leader' is used, a thinner nylon line tied between line and hook with a blood knot, and the end of this leader is called the point. Usually the last 30-45cm (12 to 18 inches), the point can also be a separate, even thinner length tied on to the leader.

point fly – in wet fly fishing, more than one fly is used on a line – traditionally three flies in a 'team'. The fly tied at the very end if the line is the point fly, those tied back from the end are called 'droppers'.

pole – a long, sectioned rod, used without a reel.

Previously called a 'roach pole', the pole can be very long, examples up to 11-12m (35 to 40ft) have been seen, and the fish is landed by withdrawing the pole backwards, travelling the hands up towards the tip. To this end, some of the very long poles are fitted with 'pole rollers'.

Another method is to dismount the pole section by section as it is pulled in.

pole pot – a swim feeder used with a pole.

pole rollers – rollers fitted to the butt end of a pole to expedite the rapid withdrawal of the rod when landing a fish.

Also seen as free-standing pieces of equipment fixed on the bank behind the pole-using angler, on which the pole is rested, permitting it to be rolled backwards.

THE COMPLEAT ANGLER
A few quotes

"In so doing, use him as though you loved him."

(instructions for baiting a hook with a live frog).

"I love any discourse of rivers, and fish and fishing."

"Angling may be said to be so like the mathematics, that it can never be fully learnt."

(From – The Epistle to the Reader – The Compleat Angler (1653)

---

pollack – *pollachius pollachius,* a member of the cod family, distributed fairly evenly around British waters, distinguishable from other members of the group by its black lateral line, whereas most have a white line.

Dark green/brown over the back of its body, fading to a creamy white or silver on the flanks and underside, these colours are variable with habitat.

Pollack live on smaller fish, feeding nearer the surface than the rest of the cod family, but will also take crustacea and shellfish. A very fast fish, it prefers the waters over reefs and wrecks, and can be taken by fish-strip or lask baits dropped down on a leger with paternosters, or by a spinning lure worked across a known pollack haunt.

Feathers or feathered jigs are also successful, and there are occasions when only a rubber eel will get results. To get the best sport, light to medium tackle is preferable, but bearing in mind the possibility of encountering other large fish in the same areas, this can result in a lot of lost gear.

However, fishing in mid-water should stay out of the way of these other monsters, and a good fight with a feisty fish should result.

> Pollack are, like the other members of the cod family, good to eat, if a little plain in flavour.
>
> They are used commercially as the bulk in the crab-flavoured, and the prawn-shaped and flavoured sea-food sticks available in most supermarkets and also fishmongers.

pollan – *coregonus pollan*, a member of the whitefish family, a branch of the salmonida, the pollan represents this genus in Ireland, being found in Lough Erne, Lough Neagh, and Lough Derg.

As they are lovers of the deeper regions of these lakes, 16-17 fathoms (100ft/30 metres), they are rarely caught by anglers, who tend not to bother with anything over 20ft, and when they are caught and brought to the surface, they have difficulty in adapting quickly to the change in pressure, thus having no energy to put up a fight.

Small fish, no more than 30cm (12in), shaped rather like a herring, (indeed, they are often referred to as the 'freshwater herring') with a blue back, silver sides and belly, they are sought after by professional fishermen, who net them in large quantities.

Their main interest to anglers is that large pike reach their enormous size by feeding upon the little pollan. All the whitefish migrate to the shallows in autumn to spawn, and it is then they are most likely to be caught.

> **pollution** – in spite of the best efforts of the National Rivers Authority, and local authorities, industrial pollution still ruins the fishing in parts of the country, and oil tankers still wash their tanks out at sea. Apart from adding to the political pressure by joining a pressure group, there is not a lot the individual can do.
>
> However, there is something each and every one of us can do – avoid contributing to the pollution yourself.

Take the rubbish home – do not leave tangles of fishing line in trees and bushes to trap birds, don't use toxic weights where non-toxic substitutes are available, don't leave your lunch bags lying around.
Observe the country-side code.

polynet – a modern micromesh net is softer than the older, knotted net that can strip mucus and scales from a fish. The latter should not now be used.

polystickle – a lure originated by the late Richard Walker, which imitates the stickleback. The 'poly' of its name comes from the clear polythene used for the body, the transparency of which emulates the body of the fish, and red and green floss are used to simulate the gut. Used for trout, and even bream have been known to take them.

pomeranian bream – once thought to be a discrete species, this is now known to be a cross between the common bream and the roach, sharing physical characteristics of both parents.

Thus, it is a deep bodied fish like the bream but with the thickness of body of the roach, and this can lead to fish of over a kilogram (2.2lb) in weight.

It can take on the colouration of either parent, or variations between them.

pools – wider, slower-moving patches of water in a river, in which fish may lie. Also, the small sweepstake bets placed between competitors in a fishing match.

poor cod – *triopterus minutus,* a small member of the cod family, resembling its large cousin save for a proportionately larger eye, this fish grows to about 20 cm (8in).

Found all around the British Isles, edible, but several are needed to make a meal. Best grilled whole, as they are hardly worth filleting.

pope – *gymnocephalus cernua,* also known as the ruffe, this little fish is a member of the percidae, and it resembles the perch in shape, if not in colouring – it is a mottled brown.

Rarely growing more than 30 cm (12in) in length, it also shares other characteristics with the perch, such as its preference for slow-moving or still waters, and its voracious feeding habits. A fish that is usually caught while fishing for other prey, the pope, though small, is as good to eat as the perch, and should be treated in the same way.

porbeagle shark – *lamna nasus,* a shark that is common all round the British Isles throughout the summer months, the porbeagle resembles the mako shark in appearance and behaviour, but is generally deeper in the body, with a tubbier shape.

If identification is difficult, it is easily resolved by looking at the teeth, which are irregular in length and disposition in the mako, but appear in neat rows in the porbeagle.

A shark of the Atlantic and Mediterranean, the porbeagle seems not to appear elsewhere in the world. It is a mid-water fish that follows schools of mackerel, after which fish it is called in some parts.

Mackerel is the obvious bait, although it will take other fish, and when it does you have a fight on your hands, and the fish needs to be played all the way into the boat.

These animals commonly grow to 190 to 200kg (420 to 440lb).

potato – part boiled potatoes threaded through so that the line passes through the middle, and slid down onto the hook, make excellent bait for large carp, once they have been acclimatised to them by liberal groundbaiting with pieces of potato over a few weeks.

Boil them just enough so that they don't fall apart when being cast. New potatoes are best, about the size that are used for canning – these are an easy but expensive way out.

poutassou – *micromesistius poutassu,* also known as the blue whiting, this fish grows to about 20cm (8in).

Found mostly around Scottish and Irish waters, less common in the English Channel, this member of the cod family prefers deep water.

> Edible, but, like the whiting, a very soft, flaky flesh, which frying does not help. Best baked or grilled.

pouting – *trisopterus luscusalso,* known as the pout-whiting, and the bib. Probably the most caught fish around British shores, this small member of the cod family is slightly coppery in colour, with faint striping like that of the freshwater perch, with a distinctive black spot in front of its pectoral fin.

Found mostly inshore, and around harbours, rocks, piers and groynes, it will take almost any bait, and is usually caught by anglers after other prey. Most caught are around the 250-500g ($1/_2$-1lb) mark, but specimens of up to 2.5kg (5lb) are found.

> Good to eat if cooked soon after capture, they are prone to rapid deterioration.
> Be prepared, however, to fight your way through a lot of bones.

pout-whiting – *see pouting.*

powan – *coregonus clupeoides,* the member of the whitefish family (a branch of the salmonidae) that represents them in Scotland, is, like the pollan, the schelly, the gwyniad and the vendace, a lover of deeper waters, and is not often caught by anglers, who rarely fish at the greater depths.

Found in Loch Lomond and Loch Esk, a small silvery fish with a bluish back, it grows to about 30cm (12in) in length. Not considered a worthy target by anglers, as when, on the rare occasions it is caught, it puts up no fight, being seemingly unable to adjust to the pressure difference on being brought quickly to the surface.

All the whitefish do come into the shallows in autumn to spawn, and this is the most likely time to catch them. The whitefish family are often known as the 'freshwater herring'.

prawns – small crustacea, easily found in rock pools at low tide – in fact, prawn fishing can be as much fun as using them to catch larger fish.

Excellent bait for a wide range of marine fish, including bass, pollack, and wrasse, and, used on a spinning rig, is as effective as the worm when salmon fishing, if a little unsporting in the eyes of some.

Prawns should be hooked near the tail, and cast gently to avoid losing them. There is also a fly tied to resemble the prawn, for those who prefer not to use the natural item.

pre-baiting – as many species of freshwater fish – mostly of the cyprinid family – spend their time moving in shoals in a pattern around their locality, seeking fish, it pays on occasion to visit the area from which you are going to fish, and throw in some bait, to get them used to the idea that this is a place where food can be found.

predation – the fact that many species of fish eat the young (and not-so-young) of their own and other species can be of use to the angler, insofar as the predator can be persuaded to take either the actual fish, caught specially for the purpose (live-baiting – for aesthetic reasons, not so popular as it was), a dead fish fished to look as if it were alive but poorly (deadbaiting), or a simulation such as a plug, spoon, fly, spinner, feathers, rubber bands.

Indeed, anything that can be made to look like a prey, and fool the quarry.

---

presentation – the manner in which the bait is offered to the fish – the variations being as infinite as your imagination.

Float-fished, legered, dapped, babbed – a wide variety of methods, and a large number of permutations of each.

What you use depends on the time, conditions, the fish you are after, the waters you are fishing, and what you have in your box.

---

priest – a short club of weighted wood, horn, bone, or metal, used to kill a fish by hitting it on the head. Hence the euphemism 'a visit from the priest'.

puffer fish – *lagocephalus laogcephalus,* a strange little warm-water fish that occasionally visits the far Southwest coasts of Britain.

It feeds on squid, and when alarmed inflates quickly to the size of a football. Reaching about 0.5kg (1lb), the puffer fish is of the same family as the fugu, the fish that the Japanese use for 'sushi'.

pumping – pulling the hooked fish nearer to the shore by raising the rod tip to the vertical, then winding in the line gained while lowering the rod.

This is repeated until the fish is within range of the landing net or gaff.

punched bread – discs of bread punched out of a sliced loaf, using a commercially available or home-made tool.

Various sizes are available – try to match the size of disc to the size of hook you are using. Will take the same types of fish that fall for bread-paste.

punt – small, flat-bottomed boat much loved by Oxbridge students for idling away summer afternoons, and a very useful fishing platform on reservoirs and slow-moving rivers. Propelled by oars or a 'quant'.

quill – the horn-like material that is the centre spine of every feather, or the spike of a hedgehog or porcupine. The feather quill and that of the porcupine are of great use as the ariel part of floats, being naturally waterproof, and easily worked.

quill minnow – a small lure in the shape of a minnow made from a quill. Used as a spinner, for trout.

quivertip – a bite indicator for use in legering, similar to the swingtip, fixed to the top of the rod.

The line is taken through the quivertip, and after being cast, is tightened so that any movement of the bait is reflected in the quivertip.

It is not unusual to find a screen or shield with lines drawn on it used in front of the rod, to act as a reference point against which movement of the quivertip can be gauged.

rabbit fish – *chimera monstrosa,* unusual-looking fish found in deeper waters, not usually caught by anglers. Growing up to about 1.5m (5ft) in length, with a tail reminiscent of that of a ray, this is an old, old species that diverged from the shark family over 400 million years ago. It still shares their cartilaginous structure.

ragworm – *neiris virens,* a marine worm, of which there are several varieties – the white rag, the maddy, the rocky, the king rag – they all make good bait, and are localised in their occurrence.

The ragworm differs very obviously from the lugworm, with a flattened body, and hundreds of leg-like protuberances along its sides, which gives us the 'rag' in its name.

Colour varies from red and green through the sandy colour of the white rag, to mostly black with a red fringe. Sizes range from the 7.5cm (3in) of the maddy, up to over 60cm (2ft) long for the king rag.

The commercially obtainable ragworm are mostly maddies, which are easily collected, as they tend to live together in little colonies, whereas the King rag, being of a solitary bent, is not so easy to find in numbers.

If you are fortunate enough to be able to collect King rags, they may be used in pieces.

Rockies will be found, as the name implies, in chalky, rocky areas, while maddies can be found in burrows or under rocks.

Be careful when hunting for or using ragworm, as they have a set of nippers at the head end, which can inflict a painful bite, which is the more painful the further away from civilisation you are fishing.

rainbow trout – *salmo gairdneri,* an introduction from the West coast of America, the rainbow seems not to breed very successfully in British waters, and needs continual restocking.

It is a tougher fish than the brown trout, which it can resemble in some of the brown's colourations, save that it has a wide streak of red along the lateral line, and is spotted all over in black, including fins and tail. Its habits differ slightly from those of its cousin, being more of a rover, and more inclined to shoaling, and it can stand murkier, less oxygenated water.

Its feeding preferences are similar, as are the methods that will catch them.

Attaining around 2 to 3kg (4.4 to 6.6lb), there are known to be some giants reaching 8kg (17+lb).

rainbow wrasse – *coris julis,* uncommon in British waters, but, nevertheless, found occasionally, this pretty fish is green, with a lighter diamond/zigzag pattern along its flanks. Like the other wrasse, it tends to take on flavours from its diet, so is unpopular as a table fish.

rays – *radiie,* rays and skates are not flatfish, which swim on their sides, with one eye migrated around so that both eyes are on one side.

Skates and rays are widened rather than flattened, with their pectoral fins enlarged into 'wings' (the part that is eaten in skates), and they swim on their bellies. They are members of the greater family that includes the sharks, and, like them, are carilaginous.

Individual species are dealt with in the appropriate places within this book.

rays bream – *brama brama,* a rare visitor to British shores, comes north in warm years. Noted for its bright silvery body and yellow fins. Not closely related to the other bream.

razorshell – razorfish, a slim, elongated shell-fish, which makes very good bait for a large number of marine fish, especially flatfish such as plaice and flounder.

Found at low tide, the razorfish retreats rapidly, going quite deep very quickly, and you have to dig fast to grab them.

Rumour has it that they will come up if salt is sprinkled down their burrows – try it! If you manage to collect more of them than you can use for bait, they make good eating for humans, too! Boil as you would any other shellfish.

record fish – the largest fish caught go into the record books – after due verification by the governing body of each branch of the sport – The N.F.A. in the case of coarse fish, the Salmon and Trout Association for game fish.

In sea angling, claims for record fish should be addressed to the British Rodcaught Fish Committee, which is administered by the N.F.S.A.

red bream – *pagellus centrodontus,* also known as the common bream, and, in Cornwall, the 'chad'.

This is a marine fish similar in shape to the black bream, but with a dark red back fading to a silvery red on the flanks and belly, with a dark patch just above and behind the gill-cover.

They will eat almost anything, and seem to prefer rough, rocky ground. Spread from the Mediterranean to the Canaries, up to Scandinavia, they are found primarily around the south-west coast of Britain.

Red bream are not large fish – 3+kg (6-7lb) – but what they lack in size, they make up in fighting spirit. Medium weight tackle will be needed, and if you catch a good-sized red bream, you have one of the tastiest fish to eat – the pinkish flesh changes to a creamy white on cooking.

When Britain and Iceland were in dispute over fishing rights in Icelandic waters, and cod was in short supply, a good deal of red bream was illicitly used as a substitute – and for sure, there are folk going around saying that cod just doesn't taste the way it used to in the 1970s.

red cod – a colour variation of the common cod, deriving from localised conditions.

red gill – a modern plastic artificial lure, very effective for pollack, coalfish, and bass.

redd – the hollow scooped out by a female salmon in which she lays her eggs.

Redditch scale – also known as the 'Old scale', this is the preferred scale for trout hooks.

red mullet – *mullus surmuletus,* this fish can be a uniform red all over, or streaked with red on a silvery background, or a pale pink with red margins around the fin areas.

Found all around the south coasts of the British Isles, and up into the North Sea off Scotland, this is a very tasty fish, much sought after in the Mediterranean, particularly around Greece.

They live on squid and shellfish, which make the ideal bait for them, and, as they feed mostly on the bottom, legering would seem the best method of catching them.

Red mullet do not grow much above 1kg (2.2lb).

redworm – an earthworm, found mainly in compost heaps, under stones and logs, and in leafmould. Up to about 8 to 10cm (3.5 to 4in long, they make good bait for the small cyprinidae.

reeds – various types of tall, grassy water-plants that grow close to the banks of lakes and slow-moving rivers, reeds have good points and bad points.

Many fish like to lurk in amongst reeds – pike use them as camouflage, others as a hiding place, so it is worthwhile casting your bait near them.

However, therein lies one of the bad points – the blighters can get in amongst the reeds, and snarl your tackle horrendously, so try to bear your quarry away from them.

Reeds, growing as they do in the shallows at the edge of a waterway, and being tall, can also be used as camouflage by the angler. Unfortunately, most seek out, and find, that neatly cleared patch that leaves a clear opening to the water, where others have fished before.

Do not forget, if anglers know about that spot, so do the fish! Do not forget, also, that fish have eyes to see, and they must be able to see anglers! Move a few yards away, and cast over the reeds.

reefs – any submerged outcropping of rock – or in tropical waters, coral – can be called a reef.

Off the north-west coast of England there are reefs of coal a few hundred feet offshore!

As they attract a wide variety of species, reefs are very popular marks for sea anglers, but the location of reefs is specialised local knowledge – take along a boatman or skipper who knows the area, and how to fish it, or your trip will be hit and miss.

Conger and ling like to live in the nooks and crannies of reefs, and wrasse and other small fish like the weeds that grow there, attracting the pollack, coalfish, cod and bass that like the little fish that like the weed.

reels – apart from the roach pole and the crab line, most methods of angling require some way of retrieving the line (with or without a fish on the end) once it has been cast out.

This is usually a mechanical device based upon the windlass, fixed to the rod at the butt end. Reels fall into two main types, with developments to the basic models, and one that is a hybridisation of the two types.

The original reels were centrepin reels, aligned fore-and-aft along the rod, with the spindle at 90° to the line of the rod, so that the line is dispensed and retrieved straight. There was no gearing, so retrieval was at a rate governed by the diameter of the central drum to which the line was attached – this could mean a lot of frantic winding.

However, owing to their simplicity of construction, ease of maintenance, and general reliability, the centrepin has, of recent years, made a comeback.

It is an ideal reel for the beginner, and a free-running centrepin is the best tool for certain kinds of angling – fly-fishing and trotting, for instance.

Most centrepin reels had an on/off ratchet provision, and some even had a drag or brake. Sizes of centrepins range from reels of 7.5 to 10cm (3 to 4in) diameter to huge machines 25 to 30cm (10 to 12in) across, see 'antiques'.

In the early 1960s, a development of the centrepin was introduced, enabling longer casts, and far quicker retrieval. This was brought about by gearing, and the reel was called a multiplier – it multiplied the number of turns made by the winding handle in relation to the drum – a ratio of 1:3 or 1:4 as common.

Other sophistications were included, such as a line distributor that laid the line evenly about the spool or drum; a 'star' drag to allow different tensions to be put upon the line; a brake; and various retarders and other gadgets incorporated to alleviate a problem common with multipliers – the 'birdsnest', a tangle caused by the over-running of the spool when the tackle has landed in the water or on the bottom.

This problem still occurs, even with all the gadgetry, and can only be prevented by the use of a thumb, lightly placed on the line when casting.

Multipliers, many of which have ball-bearings in the spindle ends, are complicated devices, and are prone to jamming if not well maintained and oiled.

At about the same time as the multiplier appeared, the fixed spool reel made its debut. In this reel, the drum around which the line is wound is at 90° to the fore-and-aft axis of the rod, and, when casting, the line spills out over the front lip, without the need for the reel to spin – hence, 'fixed spool'.

The spool is not fixed, incidentally – it moves backward and forward on retrieval, spreading the line evenly. Far greater casts are possible with this type of reel, as there are no mechanical or frictional losses.

Unfortunately, some twist is imparted to the line on casting, which is not removed on retrieval – this can lead to kinks.

Oddly enough, although the fixed spool reel looks complicated, it is far less so than the multiplier, and is quite robust, although some of the cheaper versions make use of cheap alloys (mazak) for their internal workings, which can break, or wear out.

A development of the fixed spool reel, the closed-face reel, in which the line appears from a small aperture at the front, is an improvement insofar as line control is concerned, but even this has a slight drawback – the hole through which the line emerges is by necessity small, and gives rise to a certain amount of friction, slowing the line when casting.

The hybrid type mentioned is a centrepin reel that can swivel round 90°, to act like a fixed spool for casting – there is nothing new about these reels, there are still examples around of models made in the 1930s.

They seem like a good idea, but when the line is cast, as in the fixed spool, some twist is imparted, and on retrieval, the reel being switched back to being a centrepin, more twist is imparted, making for even more kinks.

reversed quill – a quill float fished with the thin end uppermost – acting like an antenna float, giving good sensitivity with stability.

> **reservoirs** – large lakes kept for domestic and industrial water consumption, that have as a by-product a considerable angling industry.
>
> By their very nature, they are bound to contain fish – if they were not stocked artificially, nature would very soon supply a wide variety of fish. Apart from the more obvious reservoirs, there are a number of lakes throughout the country that have been adapted for this purpose, and there are a number of abandoned reservoirs that are no longer used as such.
>
> Types of fish available vary. Some reservoirs have well stocked trout fisheries, while others have a wide spectrum of coarse fish.
>
> The trout fisheries tend to have more rules and regulations, such as the types of bait or fly that can be used, restrictions on the use of boats, numbers of fish that can be taken on a permit, and so on.
>
> Coarse fish reservoirs tend to be far less regimented – you pay your money, and take your choice.
>
> Some reservoirs can be bleak places, with no trees or reeds, no cover of any sort, while others look like natural lakes – indeed, some are.
>
> Take note, however, that many reservoirs are, like gravel pits, unnatural features, so that underwater topography does not necessarily follow that of the surrounding countryside, so depth-finding can be a matter of trial and error.

roach – *rutilus rutilus,* a member of the cyprinidae, probably the most common fish of lowland waters, and the most popularly fished for by coarse fisherman, the roach is not a large fish, a 1kg (2.2lb) roach being regarded as a specimen fish.

With a slender body, slightly flattened laterally, although not so much as the bream, with a slight hump, again, not so much as the bream, the roach has a grey/green/blue back, with shiny, silvery/gold flanks, and orange lower fins, the dorsal and caudal fins being a greyish red.

The eye of the roach looks permanently bloodshot, being quite red.

Found in rivers and lakes all over Europe north of the Alps, except for the Iberian Peninsula, it is caught commercially in some parts, and is even canned. In Britain, it is not so common in the West country, and is rare in West Wales, and north of Loch Lomond.

This fish is a very tentative biter, and needs the lightest possible tackle the conditions will allow – float fishing is the most favoured method, although, as the roach will take flies off the surface on occasion, fly fishing for them is becoming more popular.

Roach do shoal with bream and chub, and will hybrize with these, and rudd. *See hybrids.*

rockling – there are two species of rockling found in British waters, *ciliata mustela,* the five-bearded rockling, and *rhinonemus cumbrius,* the three-bearded rockling.

Small members of the cod family, as the name suggests (rock + ling), they resemble the ling in shape and colouring, but only grow to about 8 to 10 inches (20 to 25 cm) in length.

The fore-part of the names derives from the fleshy barbules around the mouth, five in one case, three in the other.

rods – while bone and even metal fish hooks thousands of years old have been found by archeologists, there is no evidence for the age of the rod.

The argument that the rod was hacked from a nearby hedgerow because it so obviously enables a long cast, reaching places that cannot be reached with a hand-line does not hold water – any urchin who has ever used a crab-line will tell you that, with sufficient line looped on the ground, with a good swing around the head, a sufficiently weighted line can be propelled some distance.

A rod needs an efficient method of line storage that will not act as a drag before it becomes an efficient casting machine, and reels are, archaeologically speaking, a comparatively modern invention (the Chinese had them about the time William the Conqueror was conquering England, while they did not appear in Britain until nearly 1500).

Likewise the idea that a line tied to the end of a stick gives an advantage in reach. It becomes a limitation in the above terms. It is patently obvious that the rod (or the stick from the hedgerow) was introduced because it enables the angler to land a large fish more easily.

Anyone who has caught a fish of reasonable size on a hand-line will agree that it can be traumatic. It is true, of course, that a rod with an efficient reel will allow far greater casting distances than a well-swung hand-line.

Early rods (whenever) were probably that stick cut from the hedgerow (or bamboo row, in China), and indeed, most of what we consider modern rods were made from some sort of cane or other – either plain bamboo, or what was called 'split cane', in which a cane was split into sections down its length, and glued back together, each strip having been reversed, giving a hexagonal or octagonal cross-section. The action of the rod – the degree and position of its bendiness – being a function of its taper and length.

Bamboo and split cane rods, along with rods made from a South American wood called greenheart, held sway from Victorian times until after World War II, and the introduction of GRP (glass reinforced plastics), in which fine filaments of glass are distributed throughout a liquid resin, which is then hardened by the use of a catalyst.

GRP rods are impervious to the action of grease, oil, and seawater, and are fairly maintenance-free. They do, however, suffer from abrasion. GRP rods were originally solid affairs, made in a mould, and were relatively maintenance-free, but were somewhat dead in their action, lacking sensitivity.

This was obviated by the introduction of hollow glass rods, wound on a mandrel or metal rod, which were much easier to 'tune' by the addition or subtraction of material from different parts of the rod.

Rods made from this material probably outnumber anything else in use today, but they are being supplanted by Carbon fibre, and latterly, Kevlar, used in the same way, that is, in a resin matrix.

These latterday materials offer greater strength for lighter weight. When choosing your rod, thought must be given to the uses to which it will be put. There are 'general purpose' rods, but nowadays specialisation is more to the fore, and there is a rod for every purpose.

rod bag or rod holdall – long bag for the transport and storage of rods, bank sticks, rod rests, and any other long equipment.

rod harness – a device used in big game fishing in some parts of the world, in which a belt is taken around the shoulders of the angler, and attached to the reel, taking some of the strain from the angler's arms.

rod rest – any device designed to hold the rod in order to relieve the angler, usually in the shape of a stick or rod with a 'u' or 'y' piece at the top stuck into the bank.

rod rings – in order to make the optimum use of the 'action' of a rod, and ensure even bending, the line is run from the reel, situated on the butt or handle, up to the tip through a series of rings fixed to the rod – if the line were taken straight from the reel to the tip, it would result in a rod that bent in half at the slightest provocation.

The rings are usually of metal wire, sometimes lined with plastic or porcelain, or a clear substance known as 'agate', to allow fairly friction-free running, and are sometimes of the type that sit closely on the rod, or the type known as 'stand-off rings', which have extended legs, leaving the rings a short distance away from the body of the rod.

rod-tip legering – a method of legering used in running water, in which the tip of a normal rod (without a swing- or quiver-tip attachment) is used to indicate bites. Facing slightly down-stream, the tackle is cast, and a little time allowed for the bait and weight to sink to the bottom.

The line is then tightened, and an angle (not too big) left between the line to the rod and the bait's position, enough tension being put into the line to give a slight bend in the rod tip. Too much tension (and therefore, bend) will result in a loss of sensitivity, while too little (and a straight rod) means that if a fish lifts the bait, or swims it towards you, you will never know.

roll cast – a method of casting a fly line in confined conditions where a normal cast cannot be made.

If there are bushes, trees, or a high bank behind the caster, a normal cast will get tangled or fouled, so the roll cast is used. This entails raising the rod without taking the line off the water, and throwing it forward again, causing the line to roll in the way the a silk ribbon is twirled by a gymnast. Care must be taken to avoid rolling it over itself, causing a tangle.

roller rings – on rods that are expected to take a lot of punishment, such as deep sea fishing for large specimens, a roller is incorporated into the top ring to allow smoother retrieval and prevent the grooving that can occur in an ordinary ring.

rolling leger – a method of legering in which the weight used is a drilled bullet, through which the line is passed, held in place by small shot pinched onto the line.

As the bullet is free to rotate on the line, it can be moved about by the currents without twisting or kinking the line, and the bait appears more natural.

rotten bottom – not a reference to the state of the bed of a river, lake or the sea, but a tackle arrangement in which a lighter or weaker section of line is used to attach the weight, in places where the weight could get snagged – rocky or weedy areas.

The idea is that it is better to lose a weight (if you are fishing in an area where the likelihood of getting snagged is high, use inexpensive or disposable, and environmentally-friendly weights such as rocks, old steel nuts and bolts, etc) than all the rest of the tackle, and perhaps a fish.

round bend – a type of hook, in which the bend is a regular, wide curve, giving plenty of room for large baits, as opposed to hooks of the 'crystal' type, which have a sharper curve to the 'bend'.

> **roving matches** – angling matches in which the area or 'peg' that a competitor will fish is not set out beforehand, but decided on a draw basis – names or numbers are drawn, and the lucky ones who are drawn earlier get the first choices, those drawn last having to wait until all the others have grabbed the best places.
>
> Most sea angling matches are run on the lines of a roving match, within strict geographical limits.

rubber eels – the first lures made to imitate the sandeel were wide pieces of rubber band, or sections of rubber tubing, sometimes with metal sections incorporated, that were intended to simulate the movement of the sandeel (or a marine worm).

Commercially, these have long since given way to moulded plastic lures, but there is nothing to stop the impoverished angler making his own rubber eels.

rubbing trace – a trace of stronger material than the rest of the line, used where a rough-skinned large fish such as a shark might abrade the line while being played, or try to weaken it by dragging it across rocks – steel wire or a higher b/s nylon might be used.

rubby-dubby – a net or mesh bag holding chopped up oily fish such as herring, mackerel, and/or pilchards, trailed in the water to leave an oily, bloody wake, to attract predatory fish, primarily sharks.

rudd – *scardinius erythrophthalmus,* a fish of the cyprinidae, similar to the roach in appearance, although its body is slightly stubbier, being shorter and deeper.

Rudd grow slightly larger than roach, and the colouration is more varied, with golden/bronze flanks. The caudal, anal and pectoral fins are much redder than those of its cousin, and the dorsal fin is set slightly further back. The eye is yellowish.

The rudd is mostly vegetarian, feeding on soft water plants and algae, but they have been seen taking insects, and will take bread paste, and even maggots fished on light tackle, or, like the roach, small flies.

Rudd shoal with chub, bream and roach, and will hybridise with them. *See hybrids.*

ruffe – *gymnocephalus cerna, see pope.*

running leger (or ledger) – a leger system in which no booms are used, but hook traces are tied onto the main line, with a swivel above them, and a sliding weight above that.

SAFETY

For such a tranquil pastime, fishing is potentially a very dangerous sport. It is carried out, of necessity, in close proximity to water in large amounts. This water is often approached by slippery footpaths, down steep banks, off piers or harbour walls, or on boats – each has its dangers.

Learn to swim, take and wear buoyancy aids if on a boat, and carry flares, study safety rules and capsize/sinking drills.

If on a river bank or lakeside, do not take risks leaning over to net fish, or stand on tree-trunks, or overhangs.

If cut by a fishing knife, or impaled by a hook, take care to clean the wound with an antiseptic, which should be carried in your first-aid kit, and cover it with a suitable waterproof dressing.

Try to wash your hands before you eat those sandwiches after handling fish or any wriggling bait – you don't know where it has been!

DO TAKE CARE!

Never walk on ice. It could break under your feet.

See also first aid.

salmon – *salmo salar,* the Atlantic salmon, often called the 'king of fish', the salmon is a fish of strange migratory habits and a mysterious life-cycle.

Hatched from eggs laid in a 'redd', a hollow scooped in the gravel of the upper reaches of a stream, the young salmon or 'alevin' spends a short time – some six weeks or so – with a yolk-sac attached to its body from which it finds sustenance.

Thereafter, it must find its own food, and in doing so is vulnerable to the forces of nature – lack of food, predators, etc. The 'parr', which it is now known as, will spend two to three years in the middle reaches of the river, losing its barred parr markings, and taking on a silvery sheen, and, as a 'smolt', makes its way out to sea, where it grows enormously, increasing its weight up to 15-fold in the first year.

Where it went, and how it fed there, until recently, is all part of the mystery, for salmon were but seldom caught in commercial fishermen's trawl nets. However, we now know that a good number spend their time off Greenland, while others are known to go under the Arctic ice, safe from the depredations of the fishing industry.

After a couple of years at sea, the salmon, now known as a 'grilse', weighs up to 4.5kg (10lb), is mature enough to spawn. Some do, but many stay at sea for up to 4 or 5 years, becoming quite enormous – up to 18kg (40lb).

What urge decides the fish to return to its native river to reproduce, and when, and how it finds its way back to a particular river, we do not know. In some rivers the fish return in the autumn; in others, January; in yet others, early spring. Again, we do not know what governs this irregularity.

The last mystery is why do they allow themselves to get caught by the angler? Before moving up-river, the salmon ceases to feed. Why it should do this is not known, but nothing is ever found in the stomach of an ascending salmon.

Why then, does a salmon attack a lure that is pretending to be a fly?

The journey over, the salmon congregate in the pools of the upper reaches of the river, spawn, and some males will stay to guard the 'redds', while the females and some males will return down-river to the sea as 'kelts', and if they survive the attacks of predators in their emaciated state, return another year. In this they are unlike their Pacific cousins, who die after spawning once.

Many large tomes have been written on salmon-fishing, with advice on the best times of the year, the best methods and flies for each part of the year, how to fish each and every fly, how deep, how shallow, what part of the river, deep spinning, greased lines – it goes on and on.

Probably, more words have been written on how to catch salmon than the whole of the rest of angling altogether.

Farmed salmon are common enough in the shops for there to be no mystery about their suitability as food, and no mention need be made of the many ways to cook them. Just enjoy!

The Salmon and Trout Association is the governing body of Game fishing in the British Isles.

Address: Fishmongers' Hall, London, EC4R 9EL, and and the telephone number 0171 283 5838.

salmon flies – probably more books have been written on the salmon fly than on salmon. The size of lure, and the depth at which it is fished, are dictated by the season, the temperature, and the state of the water.

Colour is ruled by the state of the weather – the well-known saying 'a bright fly for a bright day' holds true, for bright sunlight will turn a dark lure into a black blob, while it brightens the effect of a highly coloured fly. Whether to fish them with a floating or a sinking line, use a tube fly on a treble, or a traditional fly tied on a single hook – all these decisions come with experience and tuition.

salt – the stuff that makes sea-water, as opposed to freshwater. All water running down rivers has some salt in it, picked up from the soil over which it runs, but it is concentrated in the sea.

The corrosive properties of salt are powerful, and it is essential that any reel or rod fitting used for sea fishing should be corrosion proof. Salt plus water will corrode brass, steel, aluminium, gunmetal, and chromium, and even stainless steel is not totally proof. Regular maintenance is the only answer.

sandeel – not an eel genetically, there are three species generally referred to as sandeels: the greater sandeel *hyperoplus lanceolatus,* the smooth sandeel *gymnammodytes semiquamatus,* and the sandeel *ammodytes tobianus.*

The tiny differences between these cousins is of little interest to the angler, who is only concerned that these little fish make superb bait for bass, brill, coalfish, mackerel, plaice, pollack, and turbot.

Slender, silvery fish, sandeel shoal in vast numbers – millions – by night, and lie buried in the sand by day.

They can be dug using a flat-tined fork, which will garner in a couple of hours enough for a day's fishing, or seine-netted from a rowing dinghy, which method can take enough to open a bait business.

The only difficulty in catching large numbers is that they need a good supply of oxygen – if deprived, they decline and die within minutes. Anglers of old used to keep them in a 'courge', a boat-shaped wooden box drilled full of holes, that floated behind the boat, but nowadays they can be kept in a bucket or tank, with a small aeration pump supplying the oxygen. They can, of course, be frozen for future use, and are sold in bait shops preserved in plastic bags (if these are used they benefit from an injection of pilchard oil). Usually fished – alive or dead – on a double-hooked rig, one hook through the lower lip, the other halfway down the body.

If used as live bait they need a substantial float, as they wriggle a lot.

saury pike – *scomberesox saurus,* also known as the skipper, an elongated, torpedo-shaped fish with a short beak, and its fin array well back on its body. Grows to 46 cm 18in), and feeds near the surface. Try feathers or spinners.

sausage meat – an effective, if expensive, bait. Tends to disintegrate on the hook in strong currents, but should give no trouble in still waters. Also useful as a groundbait if mixed with some cereal bait.

scad – *trachurus trachurus,* also known as the horse mackerel, the scad is shaped rather like the mackerel, but is silvery, and has a distinctive row of enlarged scales along the lateral line – it can look as though the fish has its backbone stuck on the outside.

Grows to about 1kg (2.2lb), and while it is not usually eaten by virtue of its tough skin that is hard to remove, small specimens have been caught in sprat shoals, and are eaten along with the sprats with no ill effect.

scavengers – many of the predatory fish also act as scavengers, taking carrion in many forms, apart from dead fish. They will all go for dead bait. Eels, catfish, and pike among the freshwater fish, and mackerel are the prime examples of marine scavengers.

schelly – *coregonus clupeoide pennantii,* a variety of the powan (whitefish) found in Ullswater and Haweswater in the British Lake district.

Like the other whitefish, a deepwater fish not usually angled for, but occasionally caught by accident. As with the marine wrasse, these whitefish seem to have no mechanism for pressure compensation, and become flaccid when brought to the surface quickly.

schoolies – the name given to young bass of around 0.5kg (1lb) in weight, which school together in large numbers.

sea hooks – not the marine equivalent of a sky-hook, but the business end of an angler's tackle – the part that meets the fish.

Generally larger than fresh water hooks, they are made in the same way, from high carbon content steel wire, which is not rustproof, so hooks need some minimal maintenance, such as drying off at the end of the day's fishing, sharpening to keep a sharp point, and oiling if left for any length of time unused (remember to wash the oil off before use, or use a fish oil).

Hooks are sized according to the Redditch scale, and only experience will tell you which style and size to use for which job.

Treble hooks are used far more extensively than in freshwater fishing, on different lures.

sea lice – *argulus,* a parasite that clings to salmon while they are at sea, and falls off when they enter fresh water on their spawning journey. Not an insect or a true louse, but a small crustacean.

There is no definitive evidence for the length of time the louse will live in fresh water, but it is usually taken as two days, so if the fish you catch has little nasties still clinging to it, it can be taken as being a fish fresh from the sea.

sea lochs – the long, deep inlets on the coast of Scotland, open to the sea, are called sea lochs. Similar to, although not quite as spectacular as, the fjords of Norway, they are among the most pleasurable places to fish, being as productive as the sea beyond, but more sheltered.

Salmon and sea trout, coalfish, dab and many more sea fish will be found, according to location.

$^se_as^ic_kn^es_s$

the cause of much hilarity, it is not funny when you are suffering from it, and fishing is the last thing you want to be bothered with. The unfortunate thing about the drugs that you can take to alleviate it is that they always have to be taken some time before you go aboard, and if you take them as a matter of course, you will never know if you really need them.

If possible, try a few trips without taking drugs, then you will know how bad is your own susceptibility. If you are sea-sick, try to stay above decks, think of something else (concentrate on your line!), and try to get some fluids into your stomach – if you can keep them down.

Prevention is always better than cure, so don't eat greasy foods before embarking, and stay off alcohol the night before, as a hangover is the worst possible start.

sea swivels – by their very nature, being generally larger than freshwater tackle, sea fishing rigs are more prone to twisting the line, particularly on retrieval. Thus, heavy duty swivels are needed, and are used at almost every junction between paternosters, weights, and lures.

Available in a myriad of shapes and sizes, you pays your money and takes your choice.

sea trout – *salmo trutta,* the sea-going side of the brown trout part of the salmonidae family, the sea trout was once thought to be an entirely different species, and was even called the 'salmon trout', as if it were a hybrid.

Now that scientific opinion has decided that sea trout and brown trout are the same, it could be thought that some explanation might be forthcoming about why some salmo trutta go a-wandering, while others stay at home – but no.

Sea trout follow a similar life-cycle to that of the salmon, except that their breeding season is shorter (shorter too than that of the brown trout), and the young smolts stay longer in the lower reaches of their home river, those that have been to sea returning in the autumn to spend the winter at home.

Having been at sea, the returning fish are known by various local names – finnock, sewin, peal, sprod, herling, whitling. Indeed, the name sewin is occasionally applied to the adult fish in South Wales.

The similarities between the sea trout and the salmon can cause some identification difficulty, but there are three obvious differences between the two. The trailing edge of the tail of the salmon is markedly concave, while that of the sea trout is convex, or at least straight.

The caudal peduncle (the 'wrist' in front of the tail) of the sea trout is thicker than that of the salmon – the sea trout cannot be 'tailed' by hand or with any known device.

Lastly, the maxillary bone (the bone around the upper jaw) in the sea trout extends past the eye, whereas it only reaches to the middle of the eye socket in the salmon.

The sea trout is a hardier fish than the salmon, and much more migratory, returning year after year to its native river, while the salmon, having spawned, is lucky to survive to return to the sea, and even luckier to survive to return to spawn again.

Fishing techniques are similar, although the trout seem more difficult to catch during the hours of daylight, night fishing with large, fluffy moth-like flies being the favoured ploy for this excellent fish.

Considered a pest by some purist salmon fishermen, the sea trout is a far more game fish once hooked, and in some opinions, a superior table fish. Size varies from 0.5kg to over 9kg (1-20lb) with fish over 20lb being considered specimen fish.

sectional Deal lead – a casting weight that is made in parts that are detachable from a central spine, giving a variety of weights for different conditions. The individual pieces are usually chevron-shaped, and the bottom section is diamond-shaped, the whole thing having a ribbed appearance.

self-cocking float – a float that is weighted at the bottom, so that it does not need any additional weight to cock in the water.

shad – *see Allis shad and Twaite shad.*

sharks – *pleurotremata,* this huge family of cartilaginous fishes has been around for some 70 million years without appreciable change. Included in the representatives of this group in British waters are the dogfish family, the tope, monkfish, and several that are recognisably sharks – the blue, mako, porbeagle, bramble, thresher, and six-gilled, sharks, with the hammerhead, tiger, and white sharks claimed as occasional visitors.

The cold-water loving Greenland shark is found off the Shetlands, but most of the others prefer warm waters, and are mostly found here during the summer months.

The favoured angling grounds for shark are the south west coasts of England and Ireland. One shark that is of absolutely no interest to anglers is the large basking shark, which, as a plankton feeder, cannot be tempted to take any bait the angler can present. Each of the sharks mentioned here is dealt with elsewhere in this book.

Shasta rainbow – one of the three main types of rainbow trout introduced into British waters – supposedly a non-migratory type, it has disappeared from some waters, and it is not known whether this is because it has failed to thrive, or just wandered off into feeder streams. Extremely fast-growing, very ready to take a fly, these are sought-after fish if they can be induced to stay.

shellfish – all shellfish make excellent bait for sea-fishing. Collection is usually quite easy in areas where they are prolific, often enough to make the collector forget about fishing and take a bucket of mussels home for his tea!

> **shipping forecast** – a service offered to shipping by the BBC long wave, radio 4 FM, and the World Service on short wave. As it is offered, and is free, it makes sense to use it.
>
> Angling is meant to be a source of pleasure – there is nothing pleasurable in trying to tie a hook on a line in the teeth of a gale, with the boat heaving, and water coming in green over the bows.

shock leaders – when casting heavy weights on light lines, there is a possibility that the initial snatch will put too great a strain on the line, with the risk of breakage. To obviate this, enough of a heavier gauge of line is used as a leader from the weight, to take a few turns around the reel.

shooting head – a short length of fly line, the minimum needed to get the proper action from the rod, attached to a nylon monofilament backing line, to give greater casting length, and at less cost.

> **shooting line** – not telling whoppers about the one that got away, but causing the line and the fly on the end to land gently on the water by letting out a little more line just as the lure is falling on to the surface.

short lining – a fly-fishing method used while drifting in a boat on a lake or loch.

Using a line with a tip fly and a dropper, the line is cast a short distance – 11 to 16.4m (12 to 18 yds) – and retrieved slowly, the rod tip being raised as well. When the dropper fly breaks the surface, it is retrieved more quickly, and the dropper trips across the surface from wave to wave.

This will often encourage a fish to have a go at the dropper, so the rod tip should be lowered, allowing the dropper to sink a little, so that the trout can take it.

shot position – the position of the split shot used to cock the float, and aid in casting, is dictated by the method of fishing chosen and the type and condition of the water being fished. For instance, in still water such as a lake or pond, the float will only be affected by wind, and the bait will probably rest or hang immediately below the float, so the shot can be fixed fairly closely below the float.

In moving water, the bait will be moved in the direction of flow, so shot will need to be fixed nearer the bait, to sink it quickly and keep it from being swept away.

If fishing for the type of fish renowned for 'lifting' the bait, such as bream, a couple of shot just below the float to cock it, and one or two small shot just above the bait will cause the float to rise then flatten on the surface.

Fishing 'on the drop' requires a small bunch of shot just below the float to cock it, and then a series of single shot at regular intervals along the cast, to bring the bait down to the bottom slowly.

'Back shotting', that is, using a shot or two above the float, is used to help sink the line in windy conditions.

shrimp – quite where shrimp ends and prawn begins is always problematical – indeed, in some parts of the world, what the British call prawns are referred to as shrimps – but the point as far as the angler is concerned is whether the little shellfish is big enough or small enough to fit on his hook and attract bites from the appropriate fish. Where the bait reads prawn, substitute shrimp if of a suitable size.

sidestrain – sideways pressure on a fish that is being played, to stop it getting into reed beds or amongst pier pilings, or any obstacle it could use to tangle your tackle.

silkweed – a summertime weed that is found in most rivers, in which many small life forms live, and to which, for this reason, many fish are attracted – some, indeed, feed on the weed itself. It can be used as bait for roach, chub, dace, etc., but handle it with care, so as not to disturb the little creatures hiding therein.

silver bream – *blicca bioernka,* also known as the white bream, and, as its name suggests, is of a silvery hue. It has an orange-grey-red tinge to the fins, which helps to distinguish it from its cousin, the common bream, which is also silver in its young stages, but can help to confuse it with roach/bream hybrids.

Its habits are similar to the others of its family, and the methods of catching them are the same. The silver bream is a smaller fish than the common, growing to about 1kg (2.2lb), and it occurs mostly in the east of England.

sink and draw method – a style of fishing with a dead-bait in which the bait is allowed to sink, then drawn upwards, then allowed to sink, then drawn up, simulating a sick fish, which often proves deadly for predators, particularly pike and perch.

sinker link – a short length of line to which a weight is attached.

six-gilled shark – *hexanchus griseus,* an occasional visitor to the south west coasts of England and Ireland, this is a slender shark, with, as the name suggests, six gill slits just ahead of the pectoral fins. There is no lower lobe to the caudal fin (tail), and the upper lobe is not so exaggerated as that of the thresher shark.

Grows to about 75 to 80kg (165 to 175lb).

size limits – there is no national policy on sizes of fish to be taken, but there are usually local byelaws limiting the minimum sizes of fish that may be taken – the idea is to ensure that immature fish are put back into the water to grow to maturity and breed.

There is no such obligation with marine fish, although the National Federation of Sea Anglers enforces a list of size limits during competitions run by them.

skeletons – in evolutionary terms, fishes were the first to become vertebrate – that is, to have a backbone. Thus, being first, they are less sophisticated – Mother Nature was just practising!

Also, since the skeleton of a fish has no need of a support function (the water supports the flesh of the fish), it is primarily there to give articulation, and attachment points for the muscles that provide that articulation. The bony skeleton also protects the internal organs and the backbone acts as a conduit for the spinal cord. Most fish (the so-called 'true fishes') have a calcium-containing skeleton, while the shark family and the skates and rays are cartilaginous – soft bones of 'gristle'. As they have no support function, the bones of fish need only be lightweight, and have no great strength.

slider float – a float in which the line is passed through a single eye at the bottom, and allowed to run free up to a stop-knot or a single shot pinched on the line. The float has sufficient wire wrapped around it to cock itself, and the shot on the line is just enough to sink the bait slowly.

A tell-tale shot is used near the bait, to give an indication of bites – this method seems to invite a lot of 'lift' bites.

slipping clutch – device fitted on fixed spool and multiplier reels that allows the clutch to be set at a predetermined pressure, so that a fish can take line if it pulls over a certain weight, so avoiding large fish breaking the line. The pressure can be varied at will while playing the fish. Also known as a 'drag'.

slugs – the black slug was recommended by Izaak Walton as excellent bait for the chub. A largish hook is needed (a 4 or at least a 6), through the body. Slugs can be rather large.

small-eyed ray – *raja microocellata,* a rare find, occurring off the coast of southwest England, this fish is of a greyish hue, with darker and lighter spots, and streaks. The eyes are, as the name would suggest, noticeably smaller than those of other rays, and there are spines on back and underside.

Its shape is rather like that of the thornback ray, but it generally only grows to half the size of this fish - about 5.5 to 6.5kg (12 to 14lb). As with all the other skates and rays, only the wings are eaten.

smell – a fish's sense of smell is very tied up with its sense of taste, and both are very important to it in that, mostly, they are the way it finds its food.

The mouth and any barbels are usually the organs of taste, and the nostrils above the mouth the smell organs – the combination of sensory messages these two pick up telling the fish what food is near.

It is also thought by some authorities that the salmon uses these senses to find its home river.

smelt – *osmirus eperlanus,* also known as the sparling, this little fish, up to 20 or 22cm (8 to 9 in) long, was once plentiful in estuaries on the east coast of England and Scotland, and the Shannon in Ireland.

A silvery, quick grabber of bait, it was eaten as a garnish to salmon, on account of its cucumber flavour.

smoker – small device in which oak chips are burnt, to smoke fish. These canister-type smokers are available in many tackle, camping and survival gear shops, and will usually take two or three fish.

> Trout, eels, cod, cod roe, haddock, and many other fish benefit from this method of cooking and/or preserving. Hot-smoking is the method preferred for fish that are to be eaten without further cooking. Cool- or cold-smoking is used where the fish is to be cooked before being eaten.

smolt – a salmon that has reached the stage when it leaves the river for the sea, has lost its parr markings, and is of a silvery hue.

smooth hound – *mustelus mustelus,* a member of the dogfish branch of the shark family, the smooth hound grows to about 11kg (25lb).

Its fin arrangement is similar to that of the spur dog, which is about the same size, but the smooth hound lacks the spots of its cousin, and its caudal fin is mostly on the lower edge of the upswept upper lobe, whereas the spur dog's is mostly above its straight tail.

Like the other dogfish, not something the angler goes out deliberately to catch, but edible – *see 'rock salmon'.*

snap tackle – a wire-mounted rig of two treble hooks, used for dead-baiting for pike. The wire trace is used to avoid the line being severed by the sharp teeth of the pike.

snood – the name given to a nylon hook-link on a paternoster or leger rig, or such a link made of anything other than wire.

sole – *solea solea,* commonly known as the Dover sole, probably the finest flatfish one can eat, and very expensive in the best restaurants. With its distinctive oval shape, usually a grey/brown above, white underneath, the sole is unmistakable.

It usually grows to about 1kg (2.2lb), occasionally reaching 2.5kg (5-6lb) and lives on small crustacea, marine worms, for which they forage in the muddy shallows they prefer. Use light tackle from boat or pier. Grill or poach the catch.

solenette – *microchinus boscanion,* a small sole, found mostly in the English Channel. Grows to about 13 to 15cm in length (5-6in), and is a brownish grey colour, speckled with lighter spots, and has fins of the lighter colour with streaks of the darker. Too small to eat.

South African cast – a beachcasting technique which starts with the weight or sinker laying on the ground, the rod held horizontally or beyond the horizontal, with the angler standing sideways-on to the direction of cast, his weight on the rear foot, hands well apart on the handle.

The body-weight is transferred to the other foot, the shoulders swung to face the direction of cast, and the lower hand pulls the rod butt down, the upper hand pushing upwards.

The cast is completed with the rod tip pointing at the flying sinker until it lands.

speckled trout – another name for the brook char, *salvelinus fontinalis*, an introduction from North America.

Spey cast – a double-handed salmon-fishing cast named after the Scottish river. In this, the line is lifted completely off the water and dropped into a new position.

It is a difficult cast to make, as timing is critical. Assume you are fishing from the left bank of a river, with the flow moving from your right. The fly is allowed to float downstream, and hang in the water a while, then the rod is dipped and raised over the right shoulder, and then taken in a semicircle, the fly landing slightly upstream of the angler's position.

spinner – a revolving lure that rotates around a wire core, with the assistance of vanes.

Also, the final stage in the life-cycle of a day-fly or ephemerid, after the 'dun' has shed the final skin to become the perfect fly, when it can mate. Having done this, it falls to the surface of the water as a 'spent spinner'.

> **spinning** – using a lure designed to spin quickly when dragged through the water.
>
> This is a method primarily adopted when angling for predatory fish such as perch, pike, salmon, trout, and, among marine fish, pollack, bass, coalfish, mackerel, turbot, plaice, brill, etc.

spinning vanes – a set of small, offset plastic or metal vanes which, when mounted with a built-in spike on a dead-fish bait, cause it to rotate when pulled through the water.

split cane – the preferred material for most fishing rods, and all fly rods, for many years.

Made by taking a length of cane, splitting it down its length, and gluing it back together with each piece turned inside out. This gives an octagonal or hexagonal cross-section (occasionally seen rounded off by sanding).

The merits of this form of construction are: it gives a good, all-through action to the rod, so the whole rod is involved in playing a fish: this action means that a split cane rod is consistent when casting: a wooden rod definitely feels better in the hand, and seems more responsive than modern materials.

The drawbacks include: split cane rods must never be put away wet – they warp and rot like any organic material: they can take on a 'set' or permanent bend if used to cast heavy weights frequently over long distances: split cane rods do not come self-finished – they are varnished in the factory, but, unlike glass- or carbon-fibre, they need re-varnishing at least once a year, with a flexible varnish (yacht varnish is mostly used, but the favourite among the cognoscenti was seaplane varnish, which was difficult to find): lastly, the split cane rod is heavy in comparison to rods made of modern materials.

Split cane rods are still seen on piers and riversides around the country, and it is good to see them being used, but the time is rapidly approaching when they will be collected mainly as antiques - see this entry.

split shot – small balls of various sizes, once of lead, nowadays of non-toxic metals, that are split about two-thirds the way through, to enable them to be squeezed on to the line, acting as weights.

spoon – a lure, usually of bright, polished metal, sometimes coloured, that wobbles and twists when pulled through the water. Used to imitate a sick fish, attractive to predators looking for an easy meal.

spotted ray – *raja montagui,* also known as the 'homelyn', the spotted ray is a sandy coloured fish with darker spots all over except for a margin of about 3-4cm (1-1.5ins) around the edges of the wings. It is very similar to the blond ray, except for this small difference.

Grows to about 7 to 7.5kg (15 to 16lb). Like all skates and rays, it feeds on molluscs and other crustacea, and marine worms – all of these are suitable as bait. As with the other rays and skates, the only parts that are eaten are the wings.

sprat – *sprattus sprattus,* a small silver fish related to the herring, good to eat in itself, but a dozen or so are needed to make up a meal. Excellent bait when fresh for bass, conger eel, cod, and all the dogfish family.

Found all around the coastal waters of the British Isles, and available commercially, they can be frozen for future use, but bear in mind that a thawed fish is much softer and more fragile as a hook bait.

Sprats are one of the few marine fish useful as bait in freshwater, where they make excellent bait for salmon – it used to be a common practice to preserve them in formalin, and they were sometimes coloured gold with an acriflavine solution.

spring dodger – a bite indicator made from a length of wire, stuck in the water, round which the line is passed when legering – it gives an indication of slack-line bites.

spring viraemia – also known by the acronym SVC, standing for 'Spring Viraemia of Carp' – as this viral disease usually attacks carp and other members of the cyprinidae, notably tench. It also affects catfish and pike.

The virus concerned is Rhabdovirus carpio, and does not affect humans, although it is unlikely that anyone would want to eat a fish seen to be affected – the outward symptoms of the disease including darkening of the skin, swollen eyes, abdominal swelling, paleness of the gills, protrusion of the anus, and bleeding patches on the skin and gills.

As can be deduced from the name, spring viraemia generally makes itself evident during the spring, when water temperatures rise, and mortalities occur above 7° C., the highest rates occurring at between 10 and 15° C.

Death rates decline at over 17°, and over 23° the virus has little affect, although it is known to survive. Fish can survive an attack of their virus, sometimes even without symptoms, but can still pass on the infection to fish that have not previously been exposed to the virus.

The origin of the outbreak of this disease in 1988 has not been confirmed, but imported fish stocks are suspected, and the major danger of spread is through sales and movement of infected live fish.

However, it does no harm to disinfect nets and other tackle and footwear, an iodine-based disinfectant being preferred, or a 1% solution of caustic soda (sodium hydroxide) for boots, waders, etc.

> Spring viraemia is a notifiable disease, and suspected cases should be reported without delay to the local Water Authority, or the Fish Diseases Laboratory, Ministry of Agriculture, Fisheries and Food, The Nothe, Weymouth, Dorset, DT4 8UB.
>
> Tel. 01305 206600.
>
> *A leaflet on the condition is available from this source.*

spur dogfish – *squalus acanthius,* a small member of the shark family, growing to about 7kg (15 to 16lb), the spur dog is grey coloured, with a whitish belly, and occasionally has white flecks scattered over its back and sides.

The 'spur' part of the name comes from the bony spines in front of the two dorsal fins, which are poisonous, and best avoided. It has a larger caudal fin than the other dogfish, and is far more shark-like in appearance. The flesh is as edible as the other dogfish, with the proviso that the poison glands at the base of the spines are avoided.

squatts – the maggot of the housefly, small, yellowish in colour, used mostly for groundbaiting, with the hook baited with a larger maggot, or two or more can be used on a fine-wire hook.

When used as groundbait, usually mixed with cereal groundbait.

squid – a member of the family *cephalopoda,* the squid is a mollusc with a conical body and ten tentacles, which have suckers.

All of the squid with the exception of the small wings can be used as bait, and can be frozen for future use. Squid heads are excellent bait for conger, and should be frozen separately, and kept for this purpose. Single tentacles are good bait for most flatfish and the beauty of squid is that it is a tough, rubbery meat, and stays on the hook well, and does not lose this quality after freezing.

Mostly, bait squid is bought at the fishmonger's, but occasionally it is caught on rod and line. It seems to be able to get unhooked quite easily, though, on ordinary tackle. If you are going out especially for squid, take a murderer with you – with a double row of tiny, sharp barbs, it holds squid better than anything else.

If you do catch squid this way, bear in mind that it is not much good as bait until it has lost its transparency, and become the familiar white, rubbery fish that we know, and eat in paella.

> Squid, like tripe, is a food you love or hate – no middle ground. To some it is the epitome of fishiness, to others, eating it is like chewing a rubber band. If you are of this persuasion, try the Italian way of cooking them from the Bay of Spezia – slice into very thin rings, coat in flour, then in batter (just like our beloved fish and chips!) and deep fry – the chewy squid disappears, and all that is left is the squid-flavoured crispy batter – delicious with a home-made tomato and onion sauce!

star-back reel – a centre-pin reel in which the drag or slipping clutch is controlled by a large star-shaped wheel-nut.

star drag – *see star-back reel.*

steelhead – a migratory form of the rainbow trout – it is problematical as to whether this variety has ever run British streams.

sterlet – *acipenser ruthenus,* a member of the same family as the common sturgeon, but lives entirely in fresh water, growing up to about 1.2 metres (4ft) in length, 16kg (35lb) in weight.

Similar in shape and general description to the sturgeon, with the bucklers, asymmetrical tail, and long snout. This fish is found mostly in eastern Europe and as far east as the rivers feeding the Caspian, Black, and Kara seas. It teems in the Danube.

Attempts have been made to introduce it to lakes in western Europe, where it thrives, but seems not to reproduce. It was reputed to be doing well in the Tyne-Tees region of north-eastern England.

Stewart tackle – a two- or three-hook rig for trout fishing using a worm bait, the hooks being mounted serially along a trace, rather than as a triple.

stew-ponds – in the days before fast transport that could bring fish from the ports to inland towns, freshwater fish were consumed in large numbers.

The commercial or organised side of this was the stew-pond, primarily run by and for the benefit of lords of manors and the inhabitants of monasteries. These stew-ponds were stocked with fish, which were allowed to grow to an edible size.

The main fish grown were carp, bream, tench, and in the few that had a good oxygen supply, trout.

stickleback – there are three species of sticklebacks to be found around the British Isles – the three-spined *gasterosteus aculeatus,* the nine-spined *pungitius pungitius,* and the fifteen-spined *spinachia spinachia.* These tiny fish are of great interest to aquarists and naturalists, but are of interest to anglers primarily as bait-fish.

The three-spined is found both in fresh and sea water – it grows to 5cm (2in) in fresh water, and up to about 10cm (4in) in the sea. It is probably the most widely distributed and prolific fish in British waters.

The nine-spined stickleback grow to about 7cm (2.75in) is a freshwater fish only, inhabiting similar habitats as the three-spined, but the two seem not to mix. The fifteen-spined stickleback is a marine fish, growing up to about 15cm (6in).

By its very wide distribution, the three-spined is of most interest, and there are probably more books on the subject of this fish than any other in the world.

stick float – a float made of light wood, thicker at the top than at the bottom. Gives good stability in agitated water.

Use fairly strong tackle, as the tench can be among the strongest of fighters, and your battle is likely to be among weeds and roots. They tend to feed during the evening and just after dawn, being dormant during the middle of the day and the darkest part of the night.

Although seldom eaten nowadays in the British isles, the tench was one of the fish grown in the stewponds of the middle ages, and is considered a delicacy on the Continent, the flesh being rich and tasty. Usually growing to about 2kg (4.4lb), specimen fish up to 6.8kg (15lb) are found in European waters.

There is a golden variety, specimens of which found in the wild are probably the descendants of escapees from ornamental ponds.

---

test curves, test curve loading – a fishing rod is so designed that the maximum load applied is when the line being used is exiting the rod tip at right angles to the line of the butt.

The bend of the rod is the test curve, and the amount of weight or pull required to pull the rod in this position is called the test curve loading.

The significance of this is that the pull required should be about a fifth of the breaking strain of any line used on that rod. Therefore, a rod having a test curve loading of 1kg (2.2lb) would be best used with no more than a 4.5kg (10lb) breaking strain line.

---

thermocline – water is not a very good conductor of heat – normally, heat is distributed by convection in fluids. Therefore, in summer, in any still body of water of appreciable depth, the upper layer is heated by the sun, but the lower levels stay cold.

They are separated by a thin layer of water in which there is a rapid temperature change – the thermocline. As the top and bottom layers are at different temperatures, they are of different densities so they do not intermix, and the effect continues until the upper layer's heat is lost with the onset of winter, and high winds cause the layers to mix once more.

Most of the flora and fauna of a lake will be found in the upper, warm layer.

threadline reel – an old-fashioned name for the fixed spool reel.

threadline spinning – a slightly old-fashioned term for spinning for salmon with a light-weight line – under 2.7kg (6lb) breaking strain – and a fixed spool reel.

thresher shark – *alopius vilpinus,* a moderate sized shark that is easily distinguishable by the over-sized upper lobe of its caudal fin. It feeds on mackerel, which it reputedly herds together by thrashing its tail on the surface before going in for its meal.

Growing to about 120 to 130kg (265 to 285lb), it is a beautiful blue colour, with a silvery white belly.

A fairly rare visitor to British waters, but it has been found in the upper English Channel.

---

thornback ray – *raia clavata*, also know as the roker, probably the most prolific in British waters, sold commercially as 'skate' in fish shops – the wings only being used – the thornback is easily distinguished by the patches of spines on each wing, and along its backbone.

Grey in colour, with lighter mottling, the thornback grows to 13 to 16kg 30 to 35lb). The overall shape of the 'disc' is that of a diamond, less rounded than most of the other rays. Food preference is for small fish – try sandeels for bait.

torpedo lead – a long, narrow casting lead shaped like a square edged space rocket, with the loop for attachment to the line at the blunt end.

tope – *galeorhinus galeus,* a small member of the shark family that includes the tiger shark and the dogfish, somewhat larger than the dogfish group, growing to over 30kg (65lb).

Shaped rather like the blue shark, the tope is usually a greyish, occasionally sandy colour, and can be confused with the smooth hound, as it shares a distinctive notched caudal fin.

They differ in dentition, the tope having flattened, grinding teeth.

> Worth catching for their fighting qualities, tope are, like the rest of the shark family, edible, but their most important claim to culinary fame is that they are the suppliers of the fin in the Chinese delicacy, shark's fin soup.

If fishing for tope, use a wire trace, as their teeth and rough skin will wreak havoc with a nylon line. A fine fighting fish when hooked.

topknot – *zeugopterus punctatus,* a small round flatfish with spiny scales, found all round the British Isles. Grows to about 0.5 to 0.7kg (1 to 1.5lb), and feeds on small crustacea. Usually caught while fishing for something else – plaice, for instance.

trace – the part of the line to which the hooks and weights are attached. The trace can be of lower breaking strain than the rest of the line (a 'rotten bottom'), so that if anything breaks, only the hooks and weights are lost, or it may need to be very strong, perhaps of wire, if the quarry is a fish with powerful teeth and jaws, such as a pike, skate, or shark, or if the skin of the fish might abrade it.

treble – a hook with three points, usually set at 60 degrees to each other, looking like a tiny grapnel.

trichodina – a gill parasite found in freshwater fish.

trigger fish – *balistes carolinensis,* a strange-looking fish, reminiscent of a parrot fish, that gets its name from the three erectile spines in front of its dorsal fin. These are a defence mechanism, and can be released from the locked position by pressing backwards and downwards on the rearmost spine.

Grows to about 1kg (2.2lb), and is found around most of the southern half of the British Isles, where it inhabits rocky coastal areas. Not exactly an angler's target, often caught while angling for something else.

tripping the bottom – when trotting, having the float set slightly higher on the cast than the depth of the water, so that the bait trips along the bottom. Care must be taken that the cast is not set too deep, or the bait may snag on weed or protuberance.

trolling – fishing from a moving boat, drawing the baited line behind the boat, either with a live or dead-bait, or with a spinner, spoon, or other lure. The boat can be rowed or power-driven, and it is best if two are aboard, one to row or drive, the other to tend the rods.

Rowing is probably the best method, as it causes less disturbance than power, but if one of the rare electric outboards can be obtained, its ability to go slowly and quietly makes it ideal.

trotting – a method of fishing in a river or stream, where the float tackle is allowed to follow the current, the angler following it along the bank.

trout – *salmo trutta,* the native British brown trout, including the migratory part of that family, the sea trout. As the sea trout and rainbow trout are dealt with in other parts of this book, we will deal with the brown trout here.

A member of the salmonidae, the well-known trout is among the hardest fish to describe, as it varies with location, and has until recently, often been thought to be a range of different species.

They can easily be distinguished from the rainbow trout as they lack the iridescent pink band along the sides, and their spots do not cover the fins and tail, as do those of the rainbow.

They need water with a high oxygen content, and seem to do better in chalky streams than in acid environments, where they are smaller, more wiry fish.

The average trout grows to about 2.3kg (5lb), but some cannibalistic specimen fish have reached 9kg (20lb) or more.

Some lake-bound brown trout seem to have a little of the migratory instincts of their cousins, the salmon, and their sea-trout brothers, and will ascend the feeder streams of the lake to spawn, and river trout will go up-stream for this event.

Territorial fish, they tend to feed seasonally, taking certain flies at certain times, so the angler needs to match the current diet – this is where the post-mortem comes in, the contents of the fish's stomach giving a lead as to which fly is the favourite.

Omnivores, most trout will take maggots or worms readily, but on many trout waters there is a 'fly-only' rule – whether this is to ensure good sport, or is mere snobbery, is left to the individual to decide.

tube fly – a salmon fly tied around a tube, which is slipped on to the leader before the hook is tied on, the tube being left to run free on the line above the treble hook.

The advantage of this is that the tube fly is pulled down against the hook by water pressure while being fished, but when the hook is taken and the line pulled in the opposite direction, the tube fly can ride up the line, out of the way of the fish, saving wear and tear.

The tube is usually of metal – brass or aluminium – but a plastic lining saves friction on the line. The most famous tube fly must be the 'Hairy Mary'.

tunny or tuna – *thunnus thunnus,* also known as the blue-fin, this handsome fish is a dark blue on the back, down as far as the lateral line, turning to silver then to white on the belly.

This superb fighting fish used to be caught in the North Sea as far south as the Dogger Bank, where the British record fish was taken. Tunny grow to over 360kg (800lb).

Their decline in British waters follows the decline through over-fishing of the herring shoals, upon which the tunny feeds, and the decline in the numbers of fishing vessels, which the anglers would follow in smaller boats, catching the tunny attracted by the agitation of the herring being caught in the nets.

They can still be seen in the Bay of Biscay, where they are fished by Spanish and Cornish fishermen, so if your desire to catch tunny is greater than your sense of self-preservation, and you are prepared to brave the second roughest stretch of water in the world, this is the place for you!

turbot – *scophthalmus maximus,* a large flatfish that inhabits sandy areas and the margins of gravel banks, where it feeds primarily on sandeels, although it will take other small fish.

Found largely around the south and west coasts of England, it has a wide diamond shaped body, without scales, the upper side being an olive greeny brown, mottled with darker brown patches. The underside is a creamy white.

These succulent fish grow to over 13kg (28lb), and provide excellent sport when hooked – you will need substantial tackle, say 25+lb breaking strain line, and a stout boat rod.

For bait, the sandeel is the favoured delicacy, or if live eels are not available, try strips of mackerel of herring fished to look like sandeel.

turle knot – a knot used for tying hooks to nylon, in which the hook is slipped on to the line, then a loop is made with a slip knot (a stopper knot behind this is advised), and this is slipped over the shank of the hook as it is pulled tight.

tusk – *brosme brosme,* also known as the torsk, a member of the cod family found in the North Sea, similar to the ling in shape and colouration. Grows to about 5kg (11lb), and feeds on small fish.

Squid makes a good bait for the tusk, and it ranks with the cod and ling as a table fish.

Twaite shad – *alosa fallax,* related to the Allis shad, this silvery, herring-like fish shares similar habits, penetrating rivers to the tidal limit in spring and summer to spawn. Differs from its cousin in having a line of dark smudges along the flanks, above the lateral line. Grows to about 1kg (2.2lb).

These fish have, like the Allis shad, declined in numbers through the pollution in our estuaries, where they used to give good sport, particularly falling to small spinners.

> Do not ask if they are good to eat – probably the only fish to be referred to in song by Cole Porter – *"....Waiter, bring me shad roe!...."*

UDN – ulcerative dermal necrosis, a viral disease affecting salmon. As its name implies, it is a disease that causes ulcers on the skin, the tissues in the area affected then dying.

It is thought that the virus attacks the salmon while they are at sea, and when they enter fresh water, a fungal secondary infection takes advantage of their weakened state to invade the infected parts. This gives rise to confusion of diagnosis, as there are other fungal infections that have nothing to do with UDN.

It would appear that the fish eventually dies, not as a result of the UDN, but of the secondary infection, as fish without the secondary infection seem to recover completely. The disease is supposed to affect only the salmonidae, but there is evidence of some coarse fish being affected by a similar infection, roach and perch having succumbed.

upstream casting – as a fly and its line will naturally follow the movement of a river downstream, it makes sense, to get maximum water coverage, to cast upstream of your position, allowing the bait to flow through.

vendace – *coregonus vandesius,* a small member of the whitefish family, found in some Scottish lochs and in the Lake district of Northern England. Herring-like in appearance, like other whitefish, it lives in the deeper parts of a lake, and is not often caught or even seen by anglers.

As a matter of interest, the only commercial exploitation of this little fish was during the latter part of the nineteenth and early part of the twentieth centuries, when a decoction of the scales were used to cover round glass beads, to make simulated pearls.

vibration – as fish are equipped with extremely delicate sensory organs that cover a greater range of frequencies than those of the human, vibrations play a great part in their lives.

Their perception of sound is one of interpretation of the vibrations carried to them by water, which is a better conductor of sound than air. Many fish seek their food initially by sound, and it is this that spinners, spoons, and other revolving lures seek to exploit.

Even dead-baits, fixed on spinning rigs, come into this category. Live baits, with their erratic movements, also send sound messages to predators.

The other end to this spectrum is the fear reaction of fish to unaccustomed sounds or vibrations – anyone who has tried to fish while little boys along the bank are throwing rocks at his float will tell you that fish do not hang around in such circumstances.

By the same token, the angler who trudges along the bank to his chosen spot, talking loudly to his friends, with a transistor radio blaring, dumping tackle on the ground, is doing himself no favours. Sound is transmitted through the earth into the water, and air-borne sound impinges on water – they both scare fish away. Some fish are more susceptible than others, but why take the chance?

vision, cone of – the laws of physics dictate how far out of the water a fish can see, as light impinging upon a flat transparent surface only penetrates at angles below 45 degrees – above this value it is refracted or reflected.

Thus, a fish can only see objects out of the water within a 90° cone, so if it is near the surface, it has a very restricted area of vision.

The nearer the bottom, the wider is this area, but visibility is then governed by the cleanliness or otherwise of the water.

These restrictions should be born in mind when fishing, as they can dictate how you go about your angling – if fishing a clear, shallow river, do not stand upright, announcing to all fish and sundry that you are waving this rod and line about to catch them.

Sit or crouch, and when approaching the bank, keep low, and if possible, approach from 90°, not along the bank.

Remember, also, that a fish lying deep will not see a fly on the surface as readily as one swimming near the surface, so if you know where he is, cast as accurately to him as you can.

vomerine teeth – in the family salmonidae, particularly among the trout/char cousins, colour variation sometimes makes identification problematical.

In this case, the best method of differentiation is by looking at the teeth in the upper jaw, in what are known as the vomer bones. Dentition varies insofar as numbers – the brook char has very few teeth here, the rainbow has more, curving forwards, and the brown trout has most curving backwards.

Vycoat – commercially available plastic moulding substance used to finish off the loose ends of silks, etc, when tying a fly.

waders – long rubber boots that reach up to the thighs, enabling the angler to walk into the stream or lake, reaching further with his cast.

The ordinary rubber-soled type are fine for smooth bottomed reservoirs and streams, but if rough, rocky or slippery terrain is expected, cleated or studded soles should be used.

Avoid the old-fashioned waist – or chest-high waders (these are banned in some places, anyway), as these can be dangerous – slip, go under the water, and this type can either fill with water making it difficult to stand up or swim, or can trap air, changing your centre of buoyancy, making it impossible to turn upright. If a pair of this type is all that is available, wear a stout belt cinched firmly about the waist.

As waders are made of rubber, and are easily cut or torn, it would be as well to carry some means of repair if a day's fishing is not to be ruined by an accident.

wading – taking to the water in a pair of long rubber boots or waders, in order to reach places that would ordinarily be out of reach. Care should be taken when wading in stony or slippery ground, and in waters with which you are unfamiliar. In murky water, carry some method of feeling ahead, to check the depth, and beware of underwater roots and weeds.

If walking alongside, or on dams, roll the waders down to facilitate swift jettisoning should you fall in – full waders are a definite impediment to swimming. When wading in sea-water, be sure to check, if wading at low tide, that there are no obstacles between you and high water.

waggler – an antenna float fixed to the line top and bottom, so that it waggles from side to side when checked while 'trotting'.

wagtails – lures made from spinning vanes and flat strips of rubber that flap when pulled through the water – usually home-made. Very effective for salmon, trout, sea trout, perch and pike.

walking the lead – the marine version of trotting, where the tide runs across the beach, rather that straight in and out.
The tackle, with a weight that will be moved by the current, is cast out, and the angler moves along the beach, keeping in line with it as it is swept along.

walleye – *stizostedian vitrium,* also known as the pike-perch. An introduction from America - *see pike-perch.*

wasp cake – a portion of the wasp's nest, which can be used as hook bait and as a groundbait. Collection of this material is fraught with danger, as wasps tend to defend it, and the insecticides used to kill the wasps are quite often lethal to humans, many being cyanide based.

Although many large fish have been taken on wasp cake or wasp grub baits, bear in mind that wasps do a useful job in your garden, keeping several insect pests down.
Leave them alone, and use blue-bottle maggots.

wasp grubs – the larva of the common wasp, makes excellent bait, when obtainable, for many freshwater fish, mainly chub and roach.
Tackle shops do sell them from time to time, so do not try collecting them yourself, a very dangerous pastime, given the propensity of wasps to defend themselves and their homes.

water knot – a knot used to attach a leader to the main line. The two lines are held together, alongside each other, and tied together like an overhand knot, but with several passes. This is pulled tight, and any of the trace line left above the knot is snipped off.

water rat – now referred to as the water vole. There are rats that live near water, and actually take to the water. These are distinguishable from the vole ('Ratty' of *The Wind in the Willows*) in that the lovable vole has a short, fur-covered tail, and is a rich, sleek, chocolate brown. The horrid brown rat is a scruffier individual with a hairless pink tail.

water vole – the original for 'Ratty' in *The Wind in the Willows*, the water vole is a vegetarian – in spite of the contents of the picnic basket in the book.

The worst damage this little animal can do is to river banks should his population grow too rapidly – he has to have somewhere to live!

Do not confuse him with the brown rat, some of which live near water, and are nasty, evil little pests.

Unfortunately, water voles are often killed in mistake for the brown rat. Check your identification before dispatching the suspect – the brown rat has a naked, pink tail, and he is a scruffy brown colour. The vole is a rich chocolate colour, much sleeker, and his tail is covered with fur.

water shrew – this tiny animal is decidedly not a vegetarian, unlike the water vole. Water shrews will take any small fish they can find, are strong swimmers, and hunt ferociously. Being small, they have a high metabolic rate, and have to eat all day long just to stay alive.

weather-fish – the pond loach *(see loach)*.

> **weather forecasts** – these are available on national, local, and commercial radio, all channels of television, and in newspapers. They are of interest to anglers if the angler is using a boat at sea, where a knowledge of approaching weather can be a lifesaver, and insofar as it is useful to know what clothing will be needed to stay warm and dry or cool and comfortable.

weeds – weeds can be a blessing and a nuisance. Silkweed makes excellent bait, fish lurk under and among weeds, and many types of fish spawn in weedbeds.

At the same time, weeds are an inviting place for a hooked fish to run for, and quite often a fish in the weeds is a fish lost. Even more annoying is for the tackle to get snagged on weed before there has even been a bite.

weever fish – the greater weever, *trachinus draco,* and the lesser weever, *trachinus vipera,* both have poisonous glands that discharge through the dorsal spines.

> The specimen mostly met by the bather is the lesser weever, which lies half-buried in the sand in the shallows, or even above low-water, where the unsuspecting can tread on it, thereby receiving a painful sting.
>
> The greater weever usually inhabits deeper water, but can be found in the shallows.
>
> Neither is a fish that the angler actively seeks to encounter, but they ought to be recognised, if only to save the angler a nasty shock!

The weevers are both ugly fish, with upward-facing mouths, and having long anal and dorsal fins, with the spines in front of the dorsal fin. They have yellow undersides, with reddish/brown topsides and flanks, with a grey mottling, and the dorsal fin again, yellow.

The greater weever grows to about 1kg (2.2lb), the lesser to only a few grammes. The poison injected by the weaver fish is a protein, and like, for instance, the albumen in an egg, will solidify when heated, so, if possible, immerse the wound (these are, fortunately, usually in the hand or foot) in water as hot as can be stood – this cooks the poison, so that it cannot disperse throughout the body.

weights – pieces of lead or, in the case of the smaller weights, non-toxic metals, used to keep the bait down at the level that fish are expected. Referred to as legers or leads, whatever the material.

Of course, there is absolutely no reason that weights have to be made of solid lumps of metal, or specially moulded to specific shapes – bags of stones, old nuts and bolts, or scrap metal of any sort provided they are heavy enough have all been pressed into service in cases of emergency or penury.

weirs – either natural – in which a river narrows and runs over a rocky stretch, or man-made, in places where the river takes a downward swoop. The man-made weir is used to control the flow of water through sluice gates.

The still waters above a weir are favourite places for the types of fish that like to bask, such as carp, bream, etc., and the aerated water below the weir attracts such fish as roach.

If fishing below the weir, and wading on what is known as the apron, the flat area that the water spills upon, take care, as this area can be very slippery. A favourite bait for fishing in weir areas is silkweed.

wels – another name for the catfish, originating in the Danube, introduced in some areas.

Wessex leger – simple sea-leger gear using a couple of traces and a flat lead like a capta or watch lead. Best used in harbours or off piers.

wet fly – an artificial fly for trout or salmon that is intended to sink below the surface, emulating the larval stage of a natural fly.

wheat – like hempseed, and barley, wheat, boiled until it is soft enough for the hook to penetrate, makes good bait, particularly in autumn for bream, roach, chub, rudd, and carp.

whelk – a gastropod, *bullinum,* a large shellfish of craggy appearance, with brownish, greenish grey flesh. Eaten by devotees with powerful masseter muscles, the whelk is rather chewy, and is eaten when boiled lightly (too much boiling makes them even tougher).

Much sought after in Belgium, where most of those caught in British waters end up. Makes good bait for cod if left uncooked, but a hammer is needed to extricate the animal from its shell. Neglected by anglers, but commercial fishermen use them on long-lines.

whiffing – trolling with a weighted line with two or more baited hooks on short traces. Mostly used at sea.

whipping – winding several turns of thread around an object to secure or strengthen it. Rod rings are whipped on, flies are whipped as part of their construction.

A main characteristic of whipping is that no loose ends are left – there are many ways of achieving this, all of which involve incorporating a loop of the material into the lashing, through which the loose end is passed, and pulled back under the whipping.

whiting – *merlangus merlangus*, a member of the cod family, the whiting is found all around the British Isles, and, like its cousin the pouting, is frequently caught when the angler is after other prey.

An unexciting silvery grey fish, it is not a fighter when hooked, their saving grace being that they are active when other fish seem to have gone home, and many a match has been decided on the weight of whiting caught.

Marine worms, small pieces of fish, and mussels make the best baits, and the whiting has a reputation of craftiness in taking bait off a hook before the angler has time to strike. The average weight of fish caught is around the 0.5kg (1lb) mark, but they grow up to 3kg (6.6lb).

Once considered fit only for the cat in Britain, with the decline in the cod population they are now eaten more widely. The light, white flesh has always been popular in France, where there was a fashion for frying them, floured, with the tail fixed in the mouth, as if the fish were tail-chasing – 'en colere', which translates as 'angry'. With what or whom was never explained.

If you find the flesh a little soft and flaky for frying, try baking the whiting.

whitefish – the coregonus species of herring-like freshwater fishes, including the gwyniad, powan, pollan, vendace, etc.

white skate – *raja alba,* also known as the bottle-nosed ray, the white skate is similar to the long-nosed skate, distinguished by its white underside. It will also grow larger, reaching 205kg (450lb). Found predominantly in the south western approaches of the English Channel and Irish waters.

white bream – *see silver bream.*

white marlin – *see marlin*

white ragworm – a middle sized member of the ragworm family, smaller (about 20cm (8in) long), than the king rag, fast becoming a favourite marine bait, but not available commercially because of its localised distribution.

Not so tough as the king rag, it needs delicate handling and fine wire hooks. Does not keep very well.

wide gap trout hook – a hook with a wide gap between the point and the shank, with a gentle curve twixt the two.

winders – plastic or wood frames onto which line is wound while out of use. In the days of flax or silk lines, this was an essential part of maintenance, as the lines had to be dried properly.

wind knots – unwanted knots, particularly in fly lines, caused by casting in wind. Untie these before they tighten, or they will damage the line, weakening it.

wings – the wings of natural flies are emulated by the use of pieces of feather, or hackles.

winkle – a gastropod, *littorina,* a marine relative of the garden snail, the winkle has been much favoured as a delicacy by some humans, and fish like them too. The difference is that fish prefer them uncooked.

When boiled, the winkle is easily removed from its shell by the dexterous use of a pin, but this does not work with the live animal – a hammer or a heavy boot is needed, to crack the shell.

Several winkles are needed on the hook, to make an inviting bait. The winkle is easily recognised clinging to rocks in small pools at low tide, being a small, black or brown shellfish.

winter-kill – a condition that results in the death of thousands of trout yearlings, when ice forms on a river-bed.

wire booms – paternoster and french booms for legering are usually made of wire, and stainless steel versions give least trouble.

wire lines – really strong lines used by sea-anglers for trolling at great depths or in strong currents, without having to use lead weights.

Originally introduced from America for salmon and trout in deep lakes, wire line were prone to damage through kinking, but recent innovations have obviated this and their susceptibility to corrosion, and modern lines are easy and pleasant to use.

The need for less lead weight and the lack of elasticity of wire lines means that the tackle is more sensitive, and bites are easier to feel. Drawbacks include the need to keep the line under tension at all times, to avoid kinking, and the need for stronger and more sophisticated aluminium oxide lined or roller rod rings, and stouter, larger reels – 30-35cm (12-14 ins) across.

wire traces – hook lengths made of wire, for use when after fish with sharp teeth, such as pike, conger, shark, etc, or if the skin of the fish sought is abrasive, or if the terrain over which you are fishing is likely to prove more than nylon line can stand.

witch – *glyptocephalus cynoglossus,* also known as the witch sole, this small flatfish is similar to the dab, but has no markings on the skin, and the lateral line goes straight over the pectoral fins and gill cover, without the distinctive kink of the dab. The overall shape is oval.

Good to eat, it often appears on restaurant menus as 'sole'. Prefers muddy estuaries, and is found predominantly around Irish coasts, Scotland and the North Sea, where it feeds on marine worms and small crustacea.

wood-louse – a small pill bug that rolls up to protect itself from predators. Makes a good trout bait if hooked lightly through the back, to avoid killing it. With a few of its fellows thrown into the water as an appetiser, the bug's wriggling on the surface will attract trout.

wormeries – place for keeping and cleaning up worms that have been collected for bait purposes – a boxed supply of earth and/or compost in which the worms will live happily, and perhaps even breed. This saves digging, and ensures a regular supply of bait.

Keep the wormery warm in the winter, as it will not be deep enough for the worms to burrow deep, as they do to avoid the cold.

worms – terrestrial or marine invertebrates with elongated bodies, sometimes rounded, sometimes flattened, or the larvae of certain insects. Useful as bait.

wrasse – the wrasse family is dealt with under the individual names of each member – ballan wrasse, corkwing wrasse, cuckoo wrasse, and rainbow wrasse.

wrecks – the sunken remains of ships, or, occasionally old car bodies deliberately dumped overboard to create artificial wrecks.

For some reason, perhaps because they simulate reefs, wreck sites seem to attract large fish, and are popular areas for fishing. Pollack, wrasse, conger, ling, coalfish, and bream are the predominant fish to be found around wrecks.

Being underwater, wrecks are, by their very nature, hard to find – unless you are, or have to hand, a scuba diver. Consequently, the best way to find them is to hire a boat with skipper, most of whom have their favourite marks.

Wye lead – a leger weight, slightly banana-shaped, with a distinct thickening in the middle, usually with a swivel at one end. The banana shape is to prevent the lead being rolled along in a current.

xanthochroism – scientific expression that means that a particular type of fish can have a golden variety – e.g., goldfish, a golden variety of carp.

yearling – a young salmon or trout, one year after hatching.

yellow gurnard – *trigla lucerna,* also known as the 'tub'. *See under gurnard.*

yellow trout – a colour variation of the brown trout, found in gravelly rivers or streams.

yolk-sac – the portable food supply that the alevin of the salmon or trout carries around until it is finally absorbed, between 12 and 15 weeks.

zander – *stizostedian lucioperca,* the pike-perch, an introduction from Europe. *See under pike-perch.*

zingel – *zingel zingel,* a European member of the percidae, the perch family, the zingel resembles the pike-perch in general appearance, save that it is yet more slender and streamlined, growing to about 1kg (2.2lb). Generally darker that the rest of the perches, it feeds on molluscs, crustacea, and worms. Found in the Danube and its tributaries.

zoomer – one of the many names given to a large, long antenna-type float. *See waggler.*

zulu – an artificial trout fly.

BERNARD VENABLES M.B.E.

Prolific writer and painter on angling subjects, Bernard Venables was the co-founder of the *Angling Times* in 1953 and edited it until 1962.

He created the strip-cartoon 'Mr Crabtree', serialised in the *Daily Mirror* during the 1940s, 50s and 60s, and appeared on television in the 1990s.

> ### And finally . . .
>
> Izaak Walton wrote about Sir Henry Wotton (1568-1639) as follows:
>
> ". . . he was a frequent practiser of the art of angling; of which he would say, 'it was an employment for his idle time, which was then not idly spent . . . a rest to his mind, a cheerer of his spirits, a diverter of sadness, a calmer of unquiet thoughts, a moderator of passions, a procurer of contentedness; and that it begat habits of peace and patience in those that professed and practised it'."
>
> *So there, Dr. Samuel Johnson!*

IZAAK WALTON
THE COMPLEAT ANGLER

There are probably more words, books and articles written on the subject of angling than on any other sport. Strange then, that the most popular and revered work on the subject should date from the days when catching fish on a rod and line was in its infancy as a sport.

First published in 1653, *The Compleat Angler* by Izaak Walton is unsurpassed in its advice on catching the fish discussed, and in the pleasure it gives the reader. Written for the most part as a discourse between an angler (Piscator), a hunter (Venator) and a falconer (Auceps) – with occasional intrusions by others – the book is a serene discourse upon various types of fish and the waters in which each may be caught.

Walton was born at Stafford on the 9th of August 1593, qualifying, therefore, as an Elizabethan. His father was one Jervis Walton, and of his mother nothing at all is known, not even her name. His father, for whom he was christened Izaak Filius Jervis Walton, died when he (Izaak) was three or four years old.

He went to London, probably at the age of sixteen, to be apprenticed to a trade. Which trade is problematical, for he is generally known as Izaak Walton, Mercer, and he was thought to have been apprenticed in the Haberdashery trade.

However, on his marriage to Rachel Floud in 1626, he describes himself as Izaak Walton, Ironmonger. His name does not appear on the rolls of the Haberdashers' Company, but there is an Izaak Walton in the records of the Ironmongers' Company.

Even stranger is his friendship with a number of bishops and other high-ranking clergymen and men of letters – Izaak himself was a mere tradesman, a shopkeeper, and although his father's calling is not known, the paternal grandfather is thought to have been a bailiff.

In an era in which class distinctions were rigidly drawn, such intercourse is unlikely, and Walton numbered among his close circle Dr John Donne – indeed, he was one of the small côterie at Donne's bedside when the cleric and poet died.

Izaak Walton – *continued*

Although he was to become well known through his writing – *The Compleat Angler* was but one of his works – it was an elegy to Donne after the poet's death that was his first published work.

So what was the attraction that such as Donne, Ben Johnson and Sir Henry Wotton found in Walton? Perhaps the expression found so often in reference to Walton – 'honest Izaak' gives a clue.

Certainly, the person who comes through in *The Compleat Angler* must have been an eminently likeable man – the sense of tranquillity communicates itself over three centuries.

Walton was married twice. His first wife, Rachel Floud, presented him with eight children none of whom survived infancy, and died herself shortly after the birth of the last in 1640. He retired from business life in 1643, and in 1649 married again, to Anne Ken, by whom he had one daughter and two sons, one dying young. The second Mrs Walton died in 1662.

Walton lived most of his life in London, in and around Fleet Street and Chancery Lane, with some time spent in Clerkenwell. He is known to have been living in Paternoster Row at the time of the Great Fire of London, and he rebuilt the burnt-down house in 1670.

By this time he was being referred to as 'Izaak Walton, gentleman'. He spent the latter years of his life in Winchester. He died on 15th December 1683, 90 years of age.

The Compleat Angler went through five editions in Walton's lifetime, each being an improvement or enlargement, the last being published in 1676. This edition has been reprinted more than one hundred and twenty times, and is still available today.

An appendage on trout and grayling fishing by a friend of Walton's, Charles Cotton, was added, and although this part has attracted much criticism, being written in a similar style, but without Walton's charm, it has been included in subsequent printings.

FISH CLASSIFICATION

Class Agnatha	JAWLESS FISHES	
	Order Petromyzoniformes	Lampreys *30*
	Order Myxiniformes	Hagfishes *15*
Class Chondrichthyes	CARTILAGINOUS FISHES	
	1 Elasmobranchii (Sharks and rays)	
	Order Hexanchiformes	Frilled shark, comb-toothed shark
	Order Heterodontiformes	Port Jackson sharks *10*
	Order Lamniformes	'Typical' sharks *200*
	Order Rajiformes	Skates, rays *300*
	2 Holocephali (Rabbitfishes)	
	Order Chimaeriformes	Chaimaeras, rabbitfishes *20*
Class Osteichthyes	BONY FISHES	
	1 Sarcopterygii (Fleshy-finned fishes)	
1 COELACANTHS	Order Coelacanthiformes	Coelacanth *1*
2 LUNGFISHES	Order Ceratodontiformes	Australian lungfish *1*
	Order Lepidosireniformes	S American and African lungfish *4*
	2 Actinopterygii (Ray-finned fishes)	
1 CHONDROSTEANS	Order Polypteriformes	Birchirs and reedfish *11*
	Order Acipensiformes	Paddlefish and sturgeons *25*
2 HOLOSTEANS	Order Amiiformes	Bowfin and garpikes *8*
3 TELEOSTS	Order Elopiformes	Tarpons and tenpounders *12*
	Order Anguiliformes	Eels *300*
	Order Notacanthiformes	Spiny eels *20*
	Order Clupeiformes	Herrings and anchovies *350*
	Order Osteoglassiformes	Arapaima, African butterfly fish *16*
	Order Mormyriformes	Elephant-trunk fishes, featherbacks *150*
	Order Salmoniformes	Salmon, trout, smelt, pike *500*
	Order Gonorhynchiformes	Milkfish *15*

FISH CLASSIFICATION – *continued*

Order Cypriniformes	Carp, barbs, characins, loaches *350*
Order Siluriformes	Catfishes *200*
Order Myctophiformes	Deep-sea lantern-fishes, Bombay ducks *300*
Order Percopsiformes	Pirate perches, cave dwelling amblyopsids *10*
Order Batrachoidiformes	Toadfishes *10*
Order Gobiesociformes	Clingfishes *100*
Order Lophiiformes	Anglerfishes *150*
Order Gadiformes	Cod, pollack, pearl-fishes, eelpout *450*
Order Atheriniformes	Flying fishes, toothcarps, halfbeaks *600*
Order Lampridiformes	Opah, ribbon-fishes *50*
Order Beryciformes	Squirrel-fishes *150*
Order Zeiformes	John Dory, boarfish *60*
Order Gasterosteiformes	Sticklebacks, pipefishes, seahorses *150*
Order Channiformes	Snakeheads *5*
Order Synbranchiformes	Cuchia *7*
Order Scoepaeniformes	Gurnards, miller's thumb, stonefish *700*
Order Dactylopteriformes	Flying gurnard *6*
Order Pegasiformes	Sea-moths *4*
Order Pleuronectiformes	Flatfishes *500*
Order Tatraodontiformes	Puffer fishes, trigger fishes, sun fish *250*
Order Perciformes	Perches, cichlids, damsel fishes, gobies, wrasses, parrot-fishes, gouramis, marlin, mackerel, tunny, sword-fish, spiny eels, mullets, barracudas, sea bream, croakers, ice fishes and butter-fishes *6500*

Numbers of living species in italic: e.g. Lampreys *30*